S0-AGF-440

The Tales of
PETER PARLEY
about America

BY

PETER PARLEY

FACSIMILE OF THE 1828 EDITION

WITH A NEW INTRODUCTION BY
BARROWS MUSSEY

DOVER PUBLICATIONS, INC.
NEW YORK

Copyright © 1974 by Dover Publications, Inc.
All rights reserved under Pan American and International
Copyright Conventions.

Published in Canada by General Publishing Company, Ltd.,
30 Lesmill Road, Don Mills, Toronto, Ontario.
Published in the United Kingdom by Constable and Company,
Ltd., 10 Orange Street, London WC 2.

This Dover edition, first published in 1974, is an unabridged
and unaltered republication of the 1828 enlarged edition of the
work entered in the year 1827 in the Clerk's Office of the District of Massachusetts. A new Introduction has been written
especially for the Dover edition by Barrows Mussey.

International Standard Book Number: 0-486-23046-5
(clothbound)

International Standard Book Number: 0-486-23022-8
(paperbound)

Library of Congress Catalog Card Number: 73-92876

Manufactured in the United States of America
Dover Publications, Inc.
180 Varick Street
New York, N.Y. 10014

INTRODUCTION
to the Dover Edition

DANIEL WEBSTER, returning to America from England in 1839, said there were two living Americans whom the English almost universally knew and admired. Lawyers, he said, esteemed Judge Story* of Massachusetts; and children always asked eagerly if the American visitor knew Peter Parley, who had, in Webster's phrase, "entire possession of the young hearts of old England."

The Tales of Peter Parley about America had first appeared in 1827, and a flood of new Parley

---

*Joseph Story (1779–1845) was among the most eminent legal writers of his day, an associate justice of the United States Supreme Court for 34 years.

titles was under way, so that by 1856 their creator could say he was the author or editor of 170
volumes, 116 bearing the name of Peter Parley,
with annual sales of 300,000 and a total sale of
seven million. (During his writing career the
population of the United States rose from 12.9
to 31.4 million, by way of comparison.)

Parley was born Samuel Griswold Goodrich
in the parsonage at Ridgefield, Connecticut, on
August 19, 1793, into a notable family of clergy-
men and lawyers. His grandfather Elizur Goodrich was the man who suggested to Noah Webster
that he write a dictionary; his cousin Chauncey
was Webster's son-in-law and successor as editor
of the "Unabridged."

By sixteen Samuel had met Benjamin Silli-
man, father of American chemistry and scien-
tific journalism, and been taken through Eli
Whitney's gun factory. At eighteen he found
himself working in a Hartford drygoods store.
When all hope of following other members of his
family to Yale vanished, the boy set out to edu-

cate himself with the help of George Sheldon, a publishing-house clerk two years his senior.

In the War of 1812 Samuel served six weeks as a militiaman at New London, but saw no action. Of that war he liked to remember his uncle Chauncey Goodrich's advice: "If you come to a fight, don't run away until the rest do!"

After his service young Goodrich studied French and dancing with an elderly émigré. A projected job with a New York firm in Paris evaporated in 1815 when Napoleon suddenly returned from Elba. Late that year Samuel's mentor George Sheldon set the course of his future life by taking him into a bookselling and publishing venture, which operated at Hartford from 1816 under the name of Sheldon & Goodrich.

The next decade was a hard one. The year 1816 was "eighteen-hundred-and-froze-to-death," with frost every month of the year in New England; Goodrich wrote the best account of it and published a pamphlet warning prospective emigrants to the west.

In 1817 his partner died, and Goodrich continued the business alone. Four years later he
fell from a horse, and had to spend a year on
crutches and use a cane the rest of his life (pictures of Peter Parley always show him with a
cane). His eyesight, ruined by studying French
late at night, was so weak he had to have most
books read aloud to him, and he did much of his
later writing by dictation.

Meanwhile he had married—Adeline Gratia
Bradley, a Vermont senator's daughter, in 1818.
But in June, 1822, "death entered my door, and
my home was desolate": his wife died. The
first of August his business failed. ("Fortunes,
gained and lost alternately, is supposed to have
attended his multiplied enterprises," a contemporary remembered.)

Before he folded, however, he made some ex-
periments that changed the course of American
publishing, though they brought him little or no
money. He felt, for one thing, an urge to en-

courage native authorship. The general impression in the country, he said later, was that America had no literature. This he tried to combat by issuing the venerable John Trumbull's collected poems in two handsome volumes, paying the author $1000 royalty, most of which fell as a loss on Goodrich.

Next, American history hardly existed as a subject in schools. Goodrich started his brother Charles on *A History of the United States of America,* one of the great classroom successes for many decades.

Samuel first filled out his own publishing list with a small anonymous arithmetic and a few toy-books. Then he employed eminent teachers to write textbooks of chemistry, geography, and natural philosophy according to set plans. This was the first time an American schoolbook publisher had commissioned writers to treat prescribed subjects instead of simply accepting manuscripts that came in. Goodrich thus created

the procedure now invariable in the educational
business.

Thanks to the help of his uncle Chauncey,
Goodrich, broken in health and fortune, was able
to set out in November, 1823, for a year in the
Old World—the first of what were to be 16
Atlantic crossings. "It was a great thing then,"
he wrote later, "to go to Europe and get back
safe." He docked in Liverpool after a very bad
passage of 22 days. (The shipwreck in Chapter
XII of the present volume is but the first of many
in *Parley's Tales.*)

Aside from a change of scene in Europe, Goodrich wanted to render his travels "subservient
to a desire I had long entertained of making a
reform—or at least an improvement—in books
for youth." Looking vainly for suitable works
in England, France, and Germany, he concluded
that popular education was not a subject thought
worthy of attention, or that Dilworth and Mother
Goose were the utmost that was hoped for.

There remained, however, Hannah More

(1744–1833), Horace Walpole's "Holy Hannah," who at the age of 79 still held court for some 80 visitors a day at her estate, Barley-wood near Bristol. She had been a friend of Garrick, Joshua Reynolds, and Dr. Johnson; she started as a writer of pastoral dramas, but her religious zeal led her to moral tales, tracts, ballads, essays, and other literary forms.

Goodrich, coming at the age of 12 on her *Moral Repository*, said it was the first book he read with real enthusiasm:

> The story of the Shepherd of Salisbury Plain was to me only inferior to the Bible narrative of Joseph and his brethren.*

Now he had the pleasure, "I might almost say ecstasy," of meeting his idol:

> It was in conversation with that amiable and gifted person, that I first formed the conception of the Parley Tales—the general idea of which was to make nursery books reasonable and truthful, and

---

*This quotation and those that follow are from Goodrich's *Recollections of a Lifetime* (New York and Auburn: Miller, Orton & Mulligan, 1856, 2 vols.)

thus to feed the young mind upon things whole-
some and pure, instead of things monstrous, false,
and pestilent.

(He particularly objected to the moral obliquity
of such heroes as Puss in Boots and Jack and the
Beanstalk—not without a certain justification, I
should say.)

The boy Goodrich, a bright, matter-of-fact
little Connecticut Yankee, had considered nursery rhymes beneath him. Before he read Hannah More, he said,

I regarded big books as tasks, proper for the
learned, but not fit for such as me; and little books
as nonsense, or worse than nonsense . . . As to
schoolbooks, those I had used had become associ-
ated in my memory with sitting three hours at a
time upon hard oak benches, my legs all the while
in such a cramped position that I could almost have
kicked my best friend by way of relief.

Quite willing to allow a Hawthorne or a
Charles Brockden Brown his extravagances of
imagination, he thought small children should
first be shown the world as it was. And indeed

his own work was a lot less goody-goody than Hannah More's or that of his chief American contemporary in the juvenile field, the Rev. Jacob Abbott. Considering that Goodrich counted more than a dozen parsons in his family within the degree of second cousin, I should say he preached very little.

The very name of Parley may possibly derive from Hannah More; her tract *Parley the Porter* appeared in one of his publications. But his daughter recalled hearing him mumbling the forms of the French verb *parler* in search of a name. And though the porter, like Peter, was "always talking," he was the villain of the piece. Probably the name, as usual, had several sources.

In Europe, Goodrich, always rather a tuft-hunter, sought out another idol, Sir Walter Scott; William Blackwood the publisher; Lafayette; and various others. In London he saw the first "Annual" issued by Rudolph Ackermann, a type of gift book made possible by the new steel-engraving process. Goodrich the publisher

noticed that these albums might make books
"desirable . . . presents—instead of rings, neck-
laces, shawls."

Back at home he set to work. First, in 1826,
he married Mary Boott, of a prominent Anglo-
Boston ship-owning and manufacturing family.
In October of that year he moved with his wife
to Boston, the literary metropolis of the Union,
"with the intention of publishing original works"
(i.e., not reprints) and trying his own hand at
authorship. On December 23 his son Francis
Boott Goodrich was born, and the following
February Peter Parley broke into print.

No person but his wife and one of his sisters
was admitted to the secret of what he was writing
—he was not sure of his success, for one thing;
and nursery literature did not yet command the
respect it earned after Parley's triumph.

Looking back, he reported:

When I wrote the first half-dozen of Parley's Tales,
I had formed no philosophy upon the subject. I
simply used my experience with children in addressing them . . .

He began by establishing the character of Peter Parley:

> . . . a kind-hearted old man, who had seen much of the world—and not presuming to undertake to instruct older people, loved to sit down and tell his stories to children . . .

The real innovation, probably half-conscious at the time and much too little noticed since, was the wealth of illustrations:

> I selected as subjects for my books, things capable of sensible representation, such as familiar animals, birds, trees, and of these I gave pictures, as a starting point. The first line I wrote was, "Here I am; my name is Peter Parley," and before I went further, I gave an engraving representing my hero. . . . Before I began to talk of a lion, I gave a picture of a lion . . .

For these pictures (largely wood-engravings, the most practical and economical means of printing illustrations then), Goodrich called upon the leading Boston engraver, Abel Bowen, and

his pupil George Loring Brown. Later books
were illustrated by them and various other shops.

The Tales of Peter Parley about America was
published by Carter, Hendee, & Company of
Boston on February 24, 1827. It came before
the world

> untrumpeted, and for some months seemed not to
> attract the slightest attention. Suddenly I began to
> see notices of it in the papers, all over the country,
> and in a year from the date of its publication, it
> had become a favorite.

At that point Goodrich, "complying with the
call for a new edition," produced a second, enlarged along the lines of the author's note on
page 4 of the present volume. To make the book
more useful and help get it into schools, he
divided the material into chapters, put questions
at the foot of each page, and added several cuts.
He inserted a series title page with copperplate
frontispiece—a luxury in the days when metal
engraving meant an extra printing process.

This second, enlarged edition is reproduced

in the present Dover facsimile, from its first line ("Here I am!") to the poem beginning on page 141, which must surely be the ancestor of "In fourteen hundred ninety-two/Columbus sailed the ocean blue."

The success of the *America* volume brought a series in its wake. *The Tales of Peter Parley about Europe* appeared in 1828 under Goodrich's own imprint, using some of the same woodblocks as the first volume. In 1829 came *Parley's Winter Evening Tales*; in 1830 *Parley's Juvenile Tales*, then *Parley's Asia; Africa; Sun, Moon and Stars;* and so on in a constant stream for the next 30 years. For four years, Goodrich said, he worked some 14 hours a day producing the books. With his eyesight constantly threatened, he employed others (including Nathaniel Hawthorne) to block out work for him, and dictated the final versions to his wife.

Meanwhile, with *The Token, a Christmas and New Year's Gift for 1828*, he started a series of annuals similar to those he had seen in London.

The series went on for 15 years, publishing some of the first work of Longfellow, Hawthorne, and Oliver Wendell Holmes. Another contributor was the historian George Bancroft, then Collector of the Port of Boston. Hawthorne's work in the *Token* caught his eye and earned Hawthorne an opportune custom-house job in 1838.

Goodrich also published new and old books, took over the monthly *American Journal of Education* for a year, and kept on with the Parleys. The author's identity was no longer a secret, though: Mrs. Sarah Josepha Hale revealed it in her *Ladies' Magazine* in 1830.

In 1832 Goodrich went to England for medical help with what he came to see as a psychosomatic heart ailment. While there he investigated the flourishing British imitations of his books. Thomas Tegg, a remainderman and cheap publisher, had been issuing the work of other men as Parleys, besides reprinting originals. (We must remember that no international copyright existed then or for 60 years afterward.)

Goodrich, rather than quarrel with Tegg, contracted to write new Parley volumes that could enjoy British copyright protection. Goodrich also took several of the counterfeits home with him, and even issued a couple himself. *Peter Parley's Rambles in England, Wales, Scotland, and Ireland* (Boston 1838) bears the note:

> This work is chiefly copied from the London work, which was got up in imitation of the several books which have appeared in this country . . .

Parley was far too popular in England to stop the counterfeits with a single contract, however; they continued to appear, particularly exasperating ex-Private Goodrich of the Connecticut militia when they made Peter out a loyal old British tar.

Returning from England, Goodrich moved on doctor's advice to a new house in Jamaica Plain, four miles from Boston. He lived there, and (after a bankruptcy) in the gatehouse, for more than twenty years. His publishing activities continued full blast.

In March, 1833, he launched *Peter Parley's Magazine*, a biweekly of 16 pages, 5½ x 7, using eight or nine wood-engravings. Later he sold it, later still started *Merry's Museum*, and finally incorporated the original magazine into this.

In 1837 a seven-year panic began. Goodrich was pulled under by the failure of a publishing firm he had invested in; most of the other Boston houses also suspended; but in the end Parley saved the bacon. Goodrich made stereotype plates of his new titles and rented them out to surviving publishers.

This was also a lively time for Nathaniel Hawthorne. Goodrich had recruited him for *The Token;* hired him to help with some of the Parley history titles; brought him to Boston as editorial assistant for the *American Magazine of Useful and Entertaining Knowledge* published by Goodrich's wood-engraver friend Abel Bowen and associates; suggested that he put his sketches into a book; and arranged for its publication, since Goodrich himself had abandoned publishing for writing.

Hawthorne's first, anonymous novel, *Fanshawe*, had cost him $100 and failed completely in 1826. For the volume that appeared as *Twice-Told Tales* in 1837, Hawthorne's lifelong friend Horatio Bridge provided a $250 guarantee (never needed). Said Goodrich: *"Twice-Told Tales* was deemed a failure for more than a year, when a breeze seemed to rise and fill its sails, and with it the author was carried on to fame and fortune."

Under the influence of Daniel Webster, Goodrich entered Massachusetts politics. In 1840 he also made a hundred stump speeches for William Henry Harrison as president.

In the fall of 1846 Goodrich took his family to Paris to give his children "advantages of education . . . they had been denied." Remaining in France nearly two years, they saw the revolution of February 1848 that dethroned Louis Philippe and made Louis Napoleon president.

When Vice-President Millard Fillmore succeeded Zachary Taylor as president in 1850, of course he had room for new consuls. Webster, then Secretary of State, evidently put in his oar on Goodrich's behalf. Peter Parley's creator became U.S. Consul at Paris in May, 1851.

Just as he had seen the Paris revolution of 1848, he was to see the coup d'état of 1851. On the evening of December 1, 1851, Goodrich was presented to President Louis Napoleon; the following morning the coup d'état occurred, with a good deal of unnecessary killing by the soldiers. A crowd took refuge in the courtyard of Goodrich's hotel, and at their urging he put out the Stars and Stripes—"the first and last time that I ever deemed it necessary."

In one of those reversals customary under the spoils system, Goodrich was relieved as consul when Democrat Franklin Pierce succeeded Fillmore. Despite a petition from the American colony in Paris, Goodrich was "restored to the privileges of private life" in August, 1853, but

continued to live in Paris until 1855. The same
political turnabout that ousted him made Hawthorne consul in Liverpool.

Through all these events Goodrich kept the
Parley mill grinding. His 1854 volumes *The
Wanderers by Sea and Land* and *Faggots for
the Fireside* were set, illustrated, stereotyped,
and possibly printed in Paris, though published
by Appleton in New York. Realizing, too, how
little the French knew about America, he got out
with the help of Jules Delbrück a volume of 375
pages entitled *Les Etats-Unis d'Amérique*, later
published in a Dutch edition at Amsterdam. In
1853 came *Petite Histoire Universelle*, translated
by L. E. du Buisson and the author, and *Histoire
des Etats-Unis*, both bearing the imprint of Philadelphia and Paris.

Goodrich next rented a house three miles out-
side Paris, and sat down to write *Recollections
of a Lifetime, or Men and Things I Have Seen:
in a series of familiar letters to a friend, historical, biographical, anecdotical, and descriptive.*

This memoir, finished in New York in September, 1856, is by far the best source for Goodrich's life: a historian's footnoted delight, the observation guided by a general and unegotistical curiosity. He emerges here as a man of strong but not radical convictions—firm in anti-slavery and temperance principles, yet no friend of Jeffersonian or Jacksonian democracy. Whatever the subject, he kept his head and tried to tell what happened and why.

My own notion, indeed, is that Goodrich has been forgotten because of his very virtues: first, he found a new formula for successful schoolbooks that could be imitated without genius (which he always expressly disclaimed). Able successors started from there, and Peter Parley became part of the background.

Second, his autobiography left little to add beyond the death dates of the notables who outlived him. (There has been only one book-length biography since, Daniel Roselle's of 1968.) His millions of admirers young and old died in their turn. All we can do is look at this charming facsimile and remind ourselves that even today you'll go far to find a maker of better-looking schoolbooks than S. G. Goodrich, or a taleteller with more avid listeners than Peter Parley.

Goodrich died suddenly at his home on Ninth Street, New York, on May 9, 1860. The funeral was on Sunday, May 13, at Southbury, Connecticut. All the other churches for twenty miles around were closed.

BARROWS MUSSEY

Duesseldorf 1974

A Note on Sources

Along with *Recollections* and Goodrich's own publications, I found particularly useful James Cephas Derby's enormous *Fifty Years among Authors, Books and Publishers* (New York, G. W. Carleton & Co., 1884) and Wm. J. Linton, *The History of Wood-Engraving in America*

(Boston, Estes & Lauriat, 1882). Caroline Ticknor, *Hawthorne and His Publisher* (Boston, Houghton Mifflin, 1913) touches on Goodrich in the Old Corner building.

Most particularly I must thank the American Antiquarian Society of Worcester and its director, Marcus A. McCorison, and my old friend the learned Rollo G. Silver of Boston. C. R. Eastwood of Bridgwater, Somerset, gave valuable information on Hannah More.

The Portrait

The engraving used as a frontispiece was apparently first included in *Merry's Museum,* Goodrich's second magazine, in 1850. It was definitely offered as a prize in the magazine for 1853, and was then bound in as a bonus for all the young readers. It depicts what a new acquaintance about this time described as "the Parisian dressed . . . S. G. Goodrich, with his neatly dressed and curly wig."

The Tales of
PETER PARLEY
about America

PETER PARLEY TELLING STORIES.

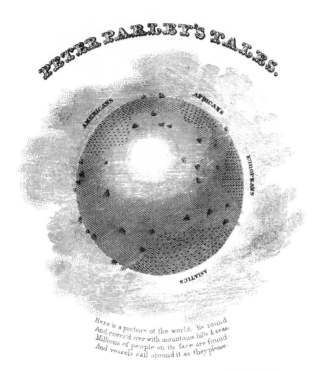

PETER PARLEY'S TALES.

AMERICANS

AFRICANS

EUROPEANS

ASIATICS

Here is a picture of the world: tis round
And cover'd o'er with mountains hills & seas:
Millions of people on its face are found
And vessels sail around it as they please.

BOSTON; CARTER, HENDEE, & COMPANY.

THE

TALES

OF

PETER PARLEY

ABOUT

AMERICA.

———

WITH ENGRAVINGS.

———

BOSTON:

CARTER, HENDEE AND CO.

DISTRICT OF MASSACHUSETTS, *to wit:*

District Clerk's Office.

BE IT REMEMBERED, that on the twenty-fourth day of February, A. D. 1827 in the fifty-first year of the Independence of the United States of America, Samuel G. Goodrich, of the said district, has deposited in this office the title of a book, the right whereof he claims as proprietor, in the words following, to wit:

"The Tales of Peter Parley about America. With Engravings."

In conformity to the act of the Congress of the United States, entitled, "An Act for the encouragement of learning, by securing the copies of maps, charts, and books, to the authors and proprietors of such copies, during the times therein mentioned;" and also to an act, entitled, "An Act supplementary to an act, entitled, An Act for the encouragement of learning, by securing the copies of maps, charts, and books, to the authors and proprietors of such copies during the times therein mentioned; and extending the benefits thereof to the arts of designing, engraving and etching historical and other prints."

JNO. W. DAVIS,
Clerk of the District of Massachusetts

PREFACE.

The design of this little work is to convey
to children, under the guise of amusement,
the first ideas of Geography and History.   In
pursuing this object, the author has connected
these grave topics with personal adventures,
and exhibited an outline merely, in simple
terms, adapted to the taste and knowledge of
children.

There is more difficulty and more importance than is generally supposed in this hum-
ble species of literature.   The *difficulty* of it
arises from the want of a language at the same
time copious enough to express a great variety
of ideas, and simple enough for the limited com-
prehension of children; the *importance* of it

lies in the powerful aid which it is capable of giving to the cause of infant education.

If the author should be thought to have been tolerably successful in this attempt to contribute something toward promoting juvenile instruction, he proposes to give a series of works of the same kind on Europe, Asia, and Africa.

———

Note to the second edition.

This work having met with very unexpected success, the author, in complying with the call for a new edition, has divided it into chapters, and added questions at the bottom of the pages, in the hope of rendering it still more useful to his young friends. It is also arranged with a view to its introduction into schools ; and, to make it more complete, several cuts have been added, and some other improvements made.

Boston, 1828.

CONTENTS.

THE

TALES OF PETER PARLEY,

ABOUT AMERICA.

TALES OF PETER PARLEY,

ABOUT AMERICA.

———◆———

CHAPTER I.

Parley tells about Himself, about Boston, and about the Indians.

1. HERE I am! My name is Peter Parley! I am an old man. I am very gray and lame. But I have seen a great many things, and had a great many adventures, and I love to talk about them.

2. I love to tell stories to children, and very often they come to my house, and they get around me, and I tell them stories of what I have seen, and of what I have heard.

3. I live in Boston. Boston is a large

town, full of houses, with a great many streets, and a great many people or inhabitants in it.

4. When you go there, you will see some persons riding about in coaches, and some riding on horseback, some running, and som walking.   Here is a picture of Boston.

5. When I was a little boy, Boston was not

half so large as it is now, and that large building, which stands very high, as you see in the picture, called the new State House, was not built then.

6. And do you know that the very place, where Boston stands, was once covered with woods, and that in those woods lived many Indians ? Did you ever see an Indian ? Here is a picture of some Indians.

Who once lived in the woods where Boston now stands ?

7. The Indians used to go nearly naked, except in winter. Their skin is not white, like ours, but reddish, or the color of copper.

8. When I was a boy, there were a great many Indians, that lived at no great distance from Boston. They lived in little huts or houses called Wigwams. Here is a picture of a Wigwam.

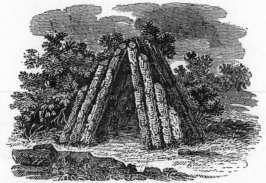

9. The Indians were very ignorant; they

How did the Indians use to go dressed?

What is the color of their skin?

What sort of houses had the Indians?

could not read or write ; their houses were very small and inconvenient. They had no such fine rooms in them as our houses have, nor had they any chimneys or fire-places.

10. The Indians had no chairs to sit in, nor tables to eat from. They had no books to read, and had no churches or meeting houses. In winter, they sometimes wore skins of bears and deer, which they shot with bows and arrows, or with guns. Here is a picture of Indians shooting a deer.

Had their houses any chimneys ?
Had they chairs or tables ?
Had they books ? Had they meeting houses or churches ?

11. There are no Indians near Boston now; they are nearly all dead, or gone far west over the mountains. But, as I said before, when I was a boy, there were a good many in New England, and they used often to come to Boston to sell the skins of wild beasts, which they had killed.

CHAPTER II.

Parley tells his Adventures.

1. When I was about twelve years old, an Indian, by the name of Wampum, came to my father's house in Boston. He had been a chief, or great man among the Indians once, but he was now poor.

2. He was generally esteemed a good

Are there any Indians near Boston now?
What has become of them?
What had Wampum been once?

Indian, and he loved my father, because he once saved his life, when he was attacked by some sailors in the streets of Boston.

3. He asked my father to let me go home with him. He told me of the excellent sport they had in shooting squirrels and deer where he lived; so I begged my father to let me go, and he at length consented.

4. Wampum lived near Northampton, at the foot of a mountain called Mount Holyoke, just on the bank of Connecticut River. It is about one hundred miles from Boston.

5. There is a good road from Boston to Northampton now, and the stage travels it every day. But the road was bad when I went with Wampum, and there were no stages in America then.

Where did Wampum live ?

How far is Mount Holyoke from Boston ?

What kind of road is there now from Boston to Northampton ?

Was it as good when Parley went with Wampum ?

6. So Wampum and I set out on foot. The second day we arrived at Worcester. It was then a very little town, and there were no such fine houses there as now.

7. The fourth day we arrived at Wampum's house, which was a little wigwam at the foot of Mount Holyoke. Here is a picture of it.

8. In this little house we found Wampum's

wife and three children; two boys and a girl. They came out to meet us, and were very glad to see Wampum and me.

9. I was very hungry and tired when I arrived. Wampum's wife roasted some bear's meat, and gave us some bread made of pounded corn, which formed our supper.

10. We sat on the floor, and took the meat in our fingers, for the Indians had no knives and forks. I then went to bed on some bear skins, and slept very well.

11. Early in the morning, Wampum called me from my sleep, and told me they were going into the woods a-shooting, and that I must go with them. I was soon ready, and set out with Wampum and his two sons.

What did Parley eat for supper at Wampum's house?
How did he sit? How did he take his meat?
What did he sleep upon?

2

CHAPTER III.

Parley tells how he went out a-shooting.

1. It was a fine bright morning in October. The sun was shining on the top of Mount Tom and Mount Holyoke, two mountains near Northampton. We ascended Holyoke through the woods.

2. At length we climbed a high rock, from which we could see the beautiful valley far below us, in the centre of which was the little town of Northampton, then much smaller than it is now.

3. "Do you see those houses?" said Wampum to me. " When my grand-father was a boy, there was not a house where you now see so many. That valley, which now belongs to white men, then belonged to the red men.

Where are Mount Tom and Mount Holyoke?
What town did Parley see from the top of Mount Holyoke?

4. " Then the red men were rich and happy; now they are poor and wretched. Then that beautiful river, which you see running through the valley, and which is called the Connecticut, was theirs.

5. " They owned these fine mountains too, they hunted in these woods, and fished in that river, and were numerous and powerful. Now we are few and weak."

6. " But how has this change happened?" said I. " Who has taken your lands from you, and made you miserable?"

7. " I will tell you all about it to-night," said Wampum, " when we return from shooting. But hark! I hear a squirrel chattering in the woods; we must go and find him. Whist!" said Wampum, " and follow me."

8. We all followed accordingly, and soon discovered a fine gray squirrel sitting in the top of a walnut tree, erect on his hind legs,

with his tail curled over his back, and a nut in his fore paws.

9. Wampum beckoned to his youngest son, who drew his bow, and discharged his arrow, which whistled over the back of the squirrel, but did not touch him.

10. Wampum's eldest son immediately discharged his arrow, which struck the squirrel in the side, and brought him instantly to the ground.

11. After this adventure, we proceeded cautiously through the woods. We had not gone far, when Wampum beckoned to us all to stop.

12. " Look yonder," said he to me, " on that high rock above us !" I did so, but could see nothing. " Look again," said Wampum. I did, and saw a young deer, or fawn, standing upon the point of a rock, which hung over the valley.

13. He was a beautiful little animal, full of spirit, with large black eyes, slender legs, and of a reddish-brown color. Here is a picture of him.

14. Wampum now selected a choice arrow, placed it on the bow, and sent it whizzing through the air. It struck the fawn directly through the heart.

15. The little animal sprang violently for-

ward over the rock, and fell dead, many feet below, where Wampum's sons soon found him. We now returned to Wampum's house, carrying the fawn with us.

———◆———

CHAPTER IV.

Parley tells how Wampum talked of his Forefathers.

1. In the evening, I reminded Wampum of his promise to tell me how the Indians had been robbed of their lands, and reduced to poverty. He accordingly began as follows:

2. "It is not a hundred and fifty years since there were no white men in this country. There were none but red men or Indians. They owned all the lands; they hunted, and fished, and rambled where they pleased.

Will you tell me what Wampum said to Parley about the white people and the Indians? If you will learn it by heart, you can say it all very easy.

3. "The woods were then full of deer and other game, and in the rivers there were a great many salmon and shad.

4. "At length, the white men came in their ships from across the sea. The red men saw them, and told them they were welcome. They came ashore. The red men received them kindly.

5. "The white men built houses, and they grew strong, and drove the red men, who had welcomed them, and whose lands they had taken, back into the woods. They killed the children of the red men, they shot their wives, they burned their wigwams, and they took away their lands.

6. "The white men had guns, the Indians had only bows and arrows. The red men fought, and killed many white men, but the white men killed more of the red men.

7. "The red men were beaten. They ran

away into the woods. They were broken-hearted, and they died. They are all dead or gone far over the mountains, except a few, and we are poor and wretched."

8. The old Indian said no more; he looked sad; his two sons looked sad also; and I almost cried, because Wampum looked so unhappy.

9. I did not understand this story very well, " but when I go back to Boston," thought I, " I will ask my grandfather about it, and he will tell me the whole story of the poor Indians."

———◆———

CHAPTER V.

Parley tells how he went to Vermont.

1. AFTER I had been at Wampum's house about a week, he told me, that he and his eldest son were going to see some Indians

in Vermont, then called New Connecticut, and I might go with them if I chose.

2. I was very happy to go, for I delighted to ramble in the woods, and to hunt squirrels and deer.

3. So we set out, crossed to the west side of Connecticut River at Northampton, and travelled along its banks, through Hatfield, Deerfield, and Greenfield.

4. We went over the very place where the beautiful town of Brattleboro' now stands. It was covered with woods, and scarcely a house was there then.

5. If you will look on a map of New England, you can trace our route.

6. After travelling three days, we arrived at what is now called Bellows Falls, about one

---

What was Vermont called when Parley went there?

What towns did Parley pass through on the banks of Connecticut River?

How far is Bellows Falls from Boston, and in what direction?

hundred and ten miles north-west of Boston, in the State of Vermont.

7. It is a wild place : the rocks are very high and rough, and the water of the Connecticut River pours over them with such fury, that it is worked into foam, and it roars like thunder.

8. I was alarmed when I first saw it whirling and boiling so furiously, and roaring so loudly, that the sight made me giddy, and the noise almost deafened me. But, by and by, I began to like the place, and to admire its strange and wild appearance.

9. Wampum told me that, in the spring of the year, the salmon, a large, fine fish, would come up the river from the sea, and ascend over the falls.

10. This must have been very difficult; but the salmon is a strong and active fish. Sometimes they would have to try several times, before they could succeed, but at length they

would spring over the rocks, and pass up the river.

11. Wampum said that the Indians were in the habit of coming in the spring, to spear the salmon as they were endeavouring to ascend the falls.

12. He described it as being excellent sport. Here is a picture of Indians spearing salmon at Bellows Falls.

___

What did Wampum say the Indians used to go to Bellows Falls for in the spring?

13. If you go to Bellows Falls now, you will find a pretty village there, and a fine bridge, from which you can see the falls, directly under you, to great advantage. But when I went there with Wampum, there were only a few small huts, or houses, and there was no bridge then.

———◆———

CHAPTER VI.

Parley continues to tell his Adventures in Vermont.

1. THE Indian village we were going to was a few miles west of Bellows Falls. We left the falls about sundown, and entered an Indian path through the woods.

2. We had not gone far before we saw a bear coming directly towards us. Wampum had a carbine in his hand, which, you know, is a short gun.

3. He levelled it at the bear, and shot it at

him. The bullet hit the bear on the head, but did not kill him. He seemed much enraged, and came fiercely towards us, growling terribly.

4. He sprung toward Wampum, striking at him forcibly with his fore paws. Wampum allowed the bear to pass him; at the same time, he plunged a knife into his side, which instantly killed him. Here is a picture of Wampum killing the bear.

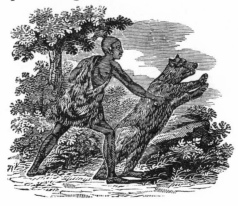

5. Soon after this, we arrived at the Indian village, which consisted of about twelve wigwams, in which were thirty or forty Indians, including women and children.

6. It was night when we arrived, and I felt alarmed to see so many Indians around me.

7. They seemed, also, to look upon me with dislike. But I felt sure that Wampum would protect me, so I was easy.

8. I was very much fatigued when I went to bed, and I fell into a deep sleep, from which I did not awake till about sunrise, when I was startled by shrieks, and shouts, and the firing of guns.

9. I instantly ran to the door, and saw the Indians running swiftly into the woods, while a party of about twenty soldiers were firing upon them.

10. The Indians soon disappeared, and the soldiers set the wigwams on fire. They made

a great blaze. Here is a picture of them
burning.

CHAPTER VII.

*Parley tells of his Return with the Soldiers, and other
Matters.*

1. THE soldiers now prepared to return to
Fort Dummer, whence they came. It was a
distance of about thirty miles, and was situated about three miles below Brattleboro', on
Connecticut River.

How far was Fort Dummer from Brattleboro' ?

2. As the soldiers expected to be pursued by the Indians, they thought it necessary to return as fast as possible, and reach the fort that night. Accordingly they set out immediately, and marched rapidly forward, taking me with them.

3. As we were going along through the woods, one of the soldiers inquired of me how I came to be among the Indians. I therefore told him my story.

4. He said that the Indians were very wicked, that they had killed a number of people, and that they assisted the French in Canada, who were then making war upon us.

5. This, you will recollect, was the period of the *French war*, (more than seventy years ago,) of which I will tell you more by and by

6. We had not proceeded far before we heard the report of a gun, and a bullet whistled over our heads. The forest was here

very thick, and we knew the Indians were around us.

7. The soldiers looked in every direction, but the cunning Indians kept themselves concealed behind the trees. Soon several guns were fired from a thicket, and one of the soldiers was wounded.

8. Looking in that direction at the moment, I distinctly saw Wampum, with his head above the bushes. At the same instant, one of the soldiers saw him also, and fired at him. I clearly saw my old protector and friend fall, and had no doubt that he was killed.

9. The Indians set up a wild and fearful yell, which seemed to startle the very trees. The soldiers took advantage of the moment, to push rapidly forward, and reached Fort Dummer in the evening.

3

CHAPTER VIII.

Parley tells about Hartford, the Charter, and Connecticut River.

1. Here I staid five or six days. I then went down the Connecticut River in a boat to Hartford. Hartford is situated on the river, and is a fine town now.

2. It was a small town then. There is a large State House there now, and an Asylum for the poor Deaf and Dumb, and a Retreat for Insane people. None of these things were in Hartford, when I was there.

3. I remember there was a house there then, standing on a hill, owned by Mr. Wyllis, the frame of which was brought from England: in front of the house, there was a large oak tree, in which the people hid the charter of Connecticut many years before.

What does Parley say of Hartford?

4. This charter was a piece of parchment, resembling paper, on which a king of England, Charles II., had written a promise that the people of Connecticut should be free.

5. When you go to Hartford you can see this charter in the Museum. But when Charles II. died, his brother, James II., became king in England.

6. Now James sent Sir Edmund Andros over to get away the charter. But the people would not let him have it, and they hid it in the old oak-tree in front of Mr. Wyllis' house.

7. You can see the tree and house too, of which I have been speaking, for they both remain to this day, although this affair occurred about one hundred and forty years ago.

What does Parley say of the charter of Connecticut ?

Who sent Sir Edmund Andros to take away the charter ?

About how long ago did Sir Edmund Andros come to get the charter of Connecticut ?

8. At Hartford, I entered on board the sloop Chenevard, and sailed for New York. We went down Connecticut River, which enters Long Island Sound about fifty miles from Hartford.

9. Connecticut River is the largest river in New England. It rises in Canada : it is about three hundred miles long, and is one of the most beautiful rivers in the world.

10. The water is clear, and the country through which it passes is delightful. You should look on a map of New England, and see the course of this fine river.

11. About eight miles from New York our sloop came very near being dashed to pieces, in what is called Hellgate, or Hurlgate.

What is the largest river in New England ?

How long is Connecticut River ?

Where does it rise ?

Where did the sloop in which Parley sailed come near being dashed to pieces ?

How far is Hurlgate from New York ?

12. This is a whirlpool, where the water is whirled around so violently, that sometimes vessels are drawn into it, and dashed to pieces on the rocks. We fortunately escaped, however, and arrived at New York.

———

CHAPTER IX.

Parley tells of New York.

1. New York is situated on an island, at the mouth of the Hudson River, and is the largest city in America. There are one hundred and sixty thousand people in it now!

2. It is three times as large as Boston. It has a fine building, called the City Hall, which is thought to be handsomer than the new State House in Boston.

What is Hurlgate?
How is New York situated?
Which is the largest city in the United States?
How many people are there in New York?
How many times is it larger than Boston?

3. When I arrived at New York, it was small compared with what it is now, but there were a great many people there then.

4. New York was first settled by Dutchmen—people who came from Holland in Europe. Dutchmen, you know, are celebrated as great smokers. Here is a picture of some Dutchmen.

Who first settled New York?
What are the Dutch celebrated for?

5. But there are people in New York from all parts of the world. I saw some French people there, the first I had ever seen. They came from France in Europe. Frenchmen are very polite. Here is a picture of a Frenchman addressing a lady.

Where do the French come from?
What sort of people are the French?

6. Here is a picture of an English gentle-
man and lady; they came from England:
there are many English people in New York,
and in other parts of America. They look
very much like Americans.

Where do the English come from?
Whom do they resemble?

7. Here is also a picture of some Spanish people, who came from Spain, in Europe. There are many of them in New York.

8. I also saw in New York some Turks, with long beards, red cloaks, and turbans on

---

Where do the Spanish come from ?

their heads.   They came from Turkey in
Europe.   Here is a picture of a Turkish gen-
tleman and lady.

9. I also saw some Chinese in New York,
who came from China, where we get tea—a
very distant country in Asia.   Here is a pic-

Where do the Turks come from ?
Where do the Chinese come from ?

ture of a Chinese pedler, selling rats and pup-
pies, for pies.

10. After staying in New York about a
month, I sailed for Boston, in the schooner
Lively, with Captain Phillips. We had a fine
wind, which carried us briskly through Long
Island Sound. Long Island Sound, you
know, is a part of the sea, which lies between

What is Long Island Sound?

Connecticut and Long Island. We stopped at Newport, a fine town in the State of Rhode Island, to leave some goods.

CHAPTER X.

Parley tells James Jenkins' Adventures.

1. At Newport, I met with a young man, several years older than myself, whom I had formerly known in Boston. His name was James Jenkins.

2. He was a roving fellow, and had just returned from a voyage to the West Indies, and had been to South America. On his way to the West Indies, he stopped at Charleston.

3. Charleston is a considerable town in South Carolina, one of the United States;

Where is Newport?
Where had James Jenkins been?
What and where is Charleston?

and is about seven or eight hundred miles south of Boston. The West Indies are a large number of islands, lying between North and South America.

4. You should look on a map, and find all the places that I mention, so that you will understand where they are situated.

5. Jenkins told me some strange stories of his adventures. I will tell you one or two of them here.

6. He sailed from Newport, Rhode Island, in the brig Yankee, with Captain Bassett. They had been at sea but a few days, when they were chased by a large French ship.

7. The French were at war with us then, and if the French ship could have taken the brig Yankee, they would have carried the

What are the West Indies?
Where do they lie?
Where did Jenkins sail from?

captain and sailors prisoners to France, and taken away their goods.

8. So the sailors of the Yankee exerted every effort to escape, and the French ship strained every nerve to come up with her. Here is a picture of the two vessels.

9. At length the French ship came near to the Yankee, and fired upon her. The cannon balls hissed through the air, and passed through the sails of the Yankee, but did no damage.

10. A second shot from the French ship

killed two men, at the very side of Jenkins.
The chase now was desperate.

11. The French ship kept an incessant fire,
and their cannon shot poured over and around
the Yankee in a shower. At this critical moment the sun went down, and night suspended the conflict.

12. Capt. Bassett took advantage of it to
escape, and in the morning was out of sight
of the French ship. In two days after this,
they arrived safe at Charleston.

13. Jenkins said he was astonished to see
so many negroes at Charleston. There are
many more negroes than white people there.

14. These negroes are slaves, and labour
for the white people, to whom they belong.
Jenkins saw negroes, men, women, and children, sold at public auction, as we sell goods.

What was Jenkins astonished to see at Charleston ?
What did Jenkins see sold at public auction at Charleston ?

15. Some of the negroes, who happen to have kind masters, are very happy; but those who have cruel masters are wretched indeed.

16. After staying a month at Charleston, the brig Yankee sailed for Cuba, the largest of the West India islands, where she soon arrived.

17. The West Indies are celebrated for producing sugar. It is made from a plant, called sugar-cane, which grows somewhat like Indian corn.

18. This is ground, and molasses is extracted from it. The sugar is found settled at the bottom of the molasses.

19. Jenkins found a great portion of the people in Cuba to be negroes. They seemed to be very gay in their disposition, and

---

Which is the largest of the West India islands?
What are the West India islands celebrated for?
What is sugar made from?

generally happy. They are very fond of dancing. Here is a picture of negroes dancing.

CHAPTER XI.

Jenkins' Adventures continued.

1. JENKINS and two of his companions, being on shore one night, were insulted by a drunken Spanish soldier. They resented it, and a scuffle ensued, in which the soldier was killed.

2. Jenkins and his two friends were apprehended for this affair, and sentenced to labour two years in the mines of Peru, in South America.

3. To this place they were soon transported, and served out the period of their sentence. Nothing could be more cruel than their situation.

4. They were obliged to work in deep pits under ground, to get out the silver ore, and were often treated with the greatest severity by their masters.

5. At length they were set at liberty, and travelled across from Peru to Brazil, that is, from the western to the eastern side of South America.

6. In performing this long journey, Jen-

Where were Jenkins and his companions sent ?
What did Jenkins and his companions have to do in the mines ?
Where did Jenkins travel when he was set at liberty ?

kins had an opportunity to see the manners of the people, and the appearance of the country.

7. Here is a picture of ladies and gen tlemen of Peru, as Jenkins described then to me.

8. There were at this time, and still are, many native Indians in South America. They have become more civilized now, but they are still an ignorant and degraded people.

What can you tell of the native Indians of South America?

Here is a picture of some of them, as Jenkins described them.

9. There is nothing in South America that strikes the beholder with so much astonishment as the Andes, a chain of mountains which run through it from north to south. They are among the loftiest mountains in the world. The highest peak, Chimborazo, is about four miles high.

What strikes the beholder with astonishment in South America?
What is the highest peak of the Andes?

10. Some of these mountains are always covered with snow, and others have fires within them, and send forth from the top a constant stream of smoke, and sometimes flame, and melted stones. These are called volcanoes. Here is a picture of some of the Andes.

11. You have heard, perhaps, of the anaconda, a very large serpent, which is found in South America. Jenkins told me the following story of one.

What can you tell of the Andes?
What is said of the anaconda?

12. A man was riding on horseback in the woods. A serpent lay coiled by the path. When the man appeared, he darted like lightning upon the horse, and wound himself around them with such force as instantly to crush them both. Here is a picture of them.

13. You have seen or heard of diamonds, bright stones, which are very valuable and precious. These are found in South America.

14. They are washed from the mountains by rains, and are found among the sand in the

Where are diamonds found?
How are they obtained?

valleys. Here are slaves employed in wash-
ing the sand for diamonds.

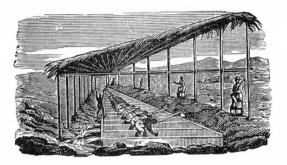

15. After a long and tedious journey on
foot, across from Peru, which is on the western coast of South America, to Brazil, which
is on the eastern coast of South America,
Jenkins and his party arrived at Rio Janeiro,
a large town in Brazil, where he embarked for
America, and arrived without further accident.

Where is Rio Janeiro ?
What is Rio Janeiro ?

CHAPTER XII.

Parley meets with Shipwreck.

1. JENKINS having finished his story, I went on board our schooner, and we soon set sail for Boston.

2. We had not been out from the harbour at Newport but a few hours, when it began to snow violently, and the wind rose till it blew a gale.

3. This wind was south-east, and therefore blew toward the shore. Lest we should be driven on the rocks, and dashed to pieces, we stretched out to sea. But the wind was too furious to allow us to carry our sails ; so we took them down, and the vessel lay to.

4. In this situation we remained for several hours. The gale, however, continually increased. I never shall forget the aspect of the

sea at that time. Its general appearance was black as ink; but the points of the waves were white with foam.

5. They rose very high, and seemed agitated with desperate fury : sometimes several of them would roll together, and dash the spray high in the air; then they would sink from the view, and leave a deep vale in the water.

6. Our little schooner danced on the ocean like a feather : now she was tossed suddenly aloft on the top of a wave ; now she slid deep into a trough formed in the sea ; now she was struck violently on the side, and nearly overset by a billow; and now she groaned and shuddered, as she was pressed on both sides by opposing waves.

7. Night at length came on; and never did I witness its approach with feelings so dreary. The storm still raged with unabated fury, and we were now drifting along at its mercy.

8. We knew the land could not be very distant, and we expected to go ashore before morning. It was an anxious night. At length the dawn appeared, but only to disclose our danger.

9. At a short distance was the shore, bound with steep and ragged rocks, and the resistless gale was bearing us furiously upon them. We gave ourselves up for lost. Some knelt down to pray; some cried aloud; and one person leaped overboard through distraction, and was drowned.

10. We soon felt the rocks grate on the bottom of the vessel. What a dreadful moment! I expected to see the vessel torn the next instant to pieces, and to be myself swallowed up in the waves.

11. At length a strong wave took the vessel on its top, and bore her along with astonishing force, and cast her high on the point of a rock.

12. What was our joy to find, that, from this position, we could leap safely upon the overhanging cliff, and escape from the danger!

13. We did so instantly, and our expectations of immediate death were in a moment exchanged for a confidence of safety. See, here is a picture of the vessel on the rocks.

14. We found the place, where we had gone ashore, to be in New Hampshire, a distance of about sixty-five miles north-east from

In what place did Parley find the schooner was driven ashore?

Boston.   From thence I travelled to Boston
on foot.

15. I was delighted to get home again, and
my family were rejoiced to see me.   I told
them my adventures, which they thought so
strange, that at first they could hardly believe
them.

CHAPTER XIII.

Parley tells about various Matters.

1. I NEED not say that I had become very
much interested in the Indians.   Wampum
had told me that once there were none but
Indians in all America ;

2. That then they owned the lands, and
were powerful and happy ; but that the white
men had got away their lands, and reduced
the Indians to weakness and misery.   I was

therefore anxious to hear the history of the Indians.

3. Beside, I had been to Northampton, Hartford, New York, and other places, and I was curious to learn more concerning them. So I asked my old grandfather, who knew all about it, to tell me the story of America. Accordingly he told it to me, and I found it very interesting.

4. But before I repeat it, I must make you understand some other things. The world, you know, is round, like a ball, or like the moon, and people go over its surface, and pass round it, just as flies creep round an apple or a pumpkin.

5. The moon looks small, because it is very far off; but it is really a great world, with mountains, and rivers, and seas upon it.

6. Now, if we were on the moon, the earth

What is the shape of the world ?

If you were on the moon, how would the world look ?

we live upon would look small and round, like the moon. Here is a picture of the world. I suppose it looks on this picture as it does to the people in the moon.

7. Well, this world, on which we live, has two great continents, or vast portions of land

on its surface; between these continents
are great oceans. On one side of the world is
America, that continent on which we live.

8. If you were high in the air, and should
sail over it, looking down, you would see that
the shape of the continent or land, called
America, is nearly the same as represented
on the following cut.

9. You see it is in two great divisions, connected by a narrow strip of land ; the northern part, on which we live, is called *North* America, and the southern part is called *South* America.

10. It is South America where almost all the gold and silver comes from. It is the country where James Jenkins was confined, as I have told you, and where, you remember, he saw the anaconda.

11. Now, on the side of the world opposite to America, is a vast continent, which is divided into Europe, Asia, and Africa. On the next page is a picture of this side of the world. Europe is represented white, Africa black, and Asia is shaded, with lines drawn across it. You must recollect that the top of the picture

---

What great continent is it we live upon ?
What is that part of America called on whicn we live ?
What part is called South America ?
Wher are Europe, Asia, and Africa ?

is north, the right hand east, the bottom south, and the left hand west. I should have told you the same of the pictures of America ; and I should inform you that the same rule applies to all maps.

Which part of a map represents north ?   Which east ?   Which south ?
Which west ?

5

12. Between these countries and America, to the east of us, lies the Atlantic Ocean, an immense sea, which is three thousand miles across.

13. On the west of America lies the Pacific Ocean, which is still broader than the Atlantic, and separates America from Asia.

14. I should like to tell you more about Asia and Africa, but I have not time now, but I will tell you about them hereafter.

15. Asia, you will remember, is the country where Adam and Eve, the first man and woman, lived, and from which the tiger is brought. On the next page is a picture of a tiger, that came from Asia.

Where does the Atlantic Ocean lie?
How far across is the Atlantic Ocean?
Where does the Pacific Ocean lie?
Which is the widest, the Atlantic or the Pacific?
Where did Adam and Eve live?
What country is the tiger brought from?

Picture of a tiger.

16. Africa is the country which negroes came from, originally, and where the leopard and ostrich are found. Here is a picture of a leopard, that came from Africa.

Where did negroes come from, originally ?
Where are the leopard and ostrich found ?

Here is a picture of an ostrich, that came from Africa.

17. Europe is the country where the English, French, Spaniards, Dutch and Russians live, about whom I have told you. But I must now tell you about Columbus.

What country is it that the English, French and Spaniards came from ?

CHAPTER XIV.

Parley tells about Columbus.

1. COLUMBUS lived in Europe. Europe is a large country, lying east of America, far over the Atlantic Ocean. You recollect it is on the picture at page 59. There are a great many people there, and many towns and cities larger than Boston or New York.

2. Well, about three hundred years ago, the people who lived on the other side of the Atlantic did not know that such a place as America existed.

3. Columbus told them that he believed there was such a place, and if they would give him some ships, he would sail across the

Where did Columbus live ?

What kind of a country is Europe ?

Where is Europe ?

What does Parley say there are in Europe ?

How long ago was it that the people on the other side of the Atlantic did not know of the existence of America ?

What did Columbus tell the people of Europe ?

water, and see if there was.   But they only laughed at him.

4. At length, Columbus persuaded the queen of Spain, whose name was Isabella, to let him have some money, with which he bought some ships, and set out to see if he could find a new country.   Here is a picture of Columbus' ships.

5. You know that people sail over the great Atlantic Ocean from Europe to America,

---

Whom did Columbus persuade to let him have some money ?
What did he do with the money he received of Isabella ?
Do people go across the Atlantic Ocean often now ?
How do they go ?

and from America to Europe, very often now. There are ships called packets, one of which sails every week from New York for England.

6. These ships are very large, and strong, and have fine rooms in them; but the time I am speaking of, about Columbus, you will re-member, was more than three hundred years ago, in the year 1492; that is, fourteen hun-dred and ninety-two years since Jesus Christ was born.

7. We call the present year 1829, because it is eighteen hundred and twenty-nine years since Jesus Christ, our Saviour, was born.

8. Well, when Columbus lived, more than three hundred years ago, the ships were small, and weak, and it was dangerous to sail in them.

What sort of ships are these packets?
How often do they sail from New York to England?
How long is it since Columbus sailed for America?
Why do we call the present year 1829?
Was it dangerous to sail in the ships in the time of Columbus?
Why was it dangerous?

9. But Columbus was a brave man, and was not afraid. So he sailed out upon the water, and soon was so far away from the land, that he could see only the sea around him.

10. He sailed along for many days, but at length a storm arose; the wind blew terribly, and the waves rose and fell violently. The ships of Columbus were tossed about, and the water dashed over them in such a manner, that the sailors, who were with Columbus were frightened, and thought they should all be drowned.

11. They begged him to go back, and threatened to kill him if he did not. But Columbus would not go back.

12. After sailing along seventy days, one of the sailors, who was on the top of the mast of

What sort of a man was Columbus?

Will you describe the storm at sea that happened when Columbus was sailing to America?

What did the sailors do?

one of the ships, saw land far over the water.
He cried, "Land! land!" Columbus was delighted. This land was America.

13. None but Indians had ever seen it before, or known that such a country existed;
Columbus and his people were the first persons from Europe who saw it and visited it.

CHAPTER XV.

Story of Columbus continued.

1. Soon after they had discovered the land,
the ships arrived along the shore. What was
the surprise of Columbus to see people on
the land, nearly naked, and of a reddish copper colour! They were very different from
any people he had ever seen.

2. These people were Indians; such as

What happened after they had sailed seventy days?

Who were the first persons from Europe who saw and visited America?

What was Columbus surprised to see?

What kind of people were the Indians?

Wampum, that I have been telling you about.
They were as much surprised to see Columbus
and his ships, as he was to see them. They
had never seen a white man or a ship before.

3. They seemed to be a kind people, for
they received Columbus with pleasure. Here
is a picture of Columbus going ashore.

What sort of people did the natives of America appear to be?
How did they receive Columbus?

4. The place, which Columbus first landed upon, was an island in the West Indies, which he called St. Salvador. He found many kinds of fruits there, which he had never seen before. After staying many days, he sailed back to Europe, and arrived at Palos, in Spain, having been absent about seven months.

5. He told the people of Europe what he had seen ; that he had discovered a new country, which abounded in delicious fruits, and silver, and gold, and the people of which, instead of being white, were red.

6. This story of Columbus made many people anxious to come to the new country, which they afterwards called America, to see

What place did Columbus first land upon ?
What did he find there ?
What did Columbus do after staying many days at St. Salvador ?
At what place did he arrive ?
What did he do on his return ?
What effect had the story of Columbus in Europe ?

what they could discover, and to get fruits, and precious metals.

7. Consequently, many persons came over, and many of them being bad and wicked men, they shot and murdered the poor Indians, destroyed their dwellings, got away their silver and gold, and took possession of their lands.

8. This was more particularly the case in South America and Mexico, which were conquered by the Spaniards, and made subject to the king of Spain.

9. I will tell you some stories relating to these countries. The most remarkable are those of Mexico and Peru.

What consequently happened ?
Where was this more particularly the case ?
What countries were conquered and made subject to the Spanish king ?

CHAPTER XVI.

Stories of Cortez and Pizarro.

1. MEXICO is on the southern part of North America. The territories subject to the emperor of Mexico were very extensive.

2. The capital of Mexico was situated in an extensive and beautiful valley, and was a large and splendid city. It was called Mexico.

3. It was by far the greatest and most interesting city in all America at the time of its discovery. The number of inhabitants was many thousands. The city still exists, and is a great place.

4. Now, the king of Spain determined to

Where is Mexico ?

Were the territories of the emperor of Mexico extensive ?

What was the capital of his empire ?

How was it situated ?

How did it compare with other towns in America at that time ?

What was the number of the inhabitants ?

What did the king of Spain determine to do ?

conquer Mexico.   The people of Mexico had
indeed done him no harm, and owed him
nothing : they were a happy and innocent
people; but this was no protection to them.

5. You will not read much about kings,
before you will learn that they care little
whether what they do is right or wrong.—
They are generally governed by selfishness,
and do what they please, without regard to
justice or humanity.

6. The person chosen to subdue Mexico
was Fernando Cortez, a cruel and desperate
man, as you will see.   He took but about six
hundred soldiers with him.

7. After several battles along the country in

Had the people of Mexico injured the king of Spain ?
What sort of people were they ?
By what are kings generally governed ?
Who was chosen to subdue Mexico ?
What sort of a man was Cortez ?
How many soldiers did he take with him ?

the way to Mexico, Cortez approached that city.

8. The emperor, who reigned at that time, was Montezuma: he received Cortez with hospitality, and treated him kindly.

9. But this did not prevent Cortez from pursuing his design : he took several men with him, suddenly entered the palace of Montezuma, seized him, and carried him away.

10. After a while, he put fetters on him, and put him in prison. In this situation Montezuma remained a long time, and suffered very ill treatment.

11. At length, the inhabitants being enraged against Cortez, to appease them, he

Who was now the emperor or king of Mexico ?

How did he treat Cortez ?

What did Cortez do ?

In what situation did Montezuma remain a long time ?

What did Cortez do to appease the inhabitants of Mexico, when they were enraged against him ?

brought Montezuma before them. But they discharged a shower of arrows at him, and Montezuma was wounded. Here is a picture of the scene.

12. The poor monarch soon died of his wounds and a broken heart. After his death, Mexico was bravely defended by his son, Guatimozin, who then became emperor.

What did the people do to Montezuma?
What became of Montezuma?
Who bravely defended Mexico after the death of Montezuma?

13. But the city was unable to hold out, and at length it surrendered to Cortez. Thus Mexico became a part of the dominions of Spain.

14. By such means, the oppression and subjugation of the weak and defenceless, kings have been accustomed to increase their wealth and power, and call it glory.

15. I will tell you another story of the same sort. A Spaniard, by the name of Pizarro, discovered Peru; a country in South America, celebrated for its mines of gold and silver. It is the same country where James Jenkins, that I told you of, was confined.

16. Pizarro having discovered this country, he resolved to conquer it. By artifice,

Did Mexico surrender to Cortez?
To what kingdom did Mexico become annexed?
Who discovered Peru?
What is Peru celebrated for?
By what means did Pizarro make Atahualpa prisoner?

6

he at length succeeded in making Atahualpa, one of the Indian chiefs, his prisoner.

17. He offered to let him go, if he would pay him a large sum of gold. This Atahualpa did. But Pizarro, instead of fulfilling his promise, burnt him to death! Such is the work of conquerors! Here is a picture of the death of Atahualpa.

18. Pizarro then pursued his conquest, and

How did Pizarro treat Atahualpa?
What then did Pizarro do?

succeeded in subjugating the whole of Peru in
1532. He then established laws for the
country, and laid the foundation of the present
town of Lima, which you will find on the
maps of South America. But in 1541 he
was murdered.

19. I have now told you some of the most
remarkable events which took place in South
America. I will now tell you some stories
of North America.

———◆———

CHAPTER XVII.

Parley tells about the Settlement of North America.

1. About two hundred and twenty years
ago, that is, in the year 1607, some English
people, about one hundred in number, came

———

What town did Pizarro lay the foundation of?
What was Pizarro's fate?
When, and by whom, was the first settlement made in Virginia?

to Virginia, and made a settlement on James
River.

2. The first town they built they called
Jamestown.   Here is a picture of the building
of Jamestown.

3. I need not tell you, that no people but

Indians lived in this part of North America at this time.

4. The great towns, such as Boston, New York, Philadelphia and others, did not exist then.

5. Vast forests extended over the whole country, and in these forests lived numerous tribes of Indians.

6. These Indians were generally unfriendly to the white people, and would often kill them, if they could.

7. One day, Captain Smith, who was one of the people of Jamestown, had been up a river in a boat. He was discovered by the Indians, seized by them, and carried before Powhattan, who was their chief, or king.

8. Powhattan and his counsellors decided

What towns did not exist at the time we are speaking of?
What was the state of the country then?
Will you tell the story of Captain Smith?

that he should be put to death. Accordingly, he was brought forward, and his head laid upon a stone. Powhattan then took a club, and raised it in the air, to strike the fatal blow.

9. What was his astonishment, to see his daughter, a beautiful Indian girl, run shrieking between him and Smith, and place herself in a situation to shelter him from the club of her father !   Here is a picture of the scene.

10. Powhattan was so much moved by the conduct of his charming daughter, who thus taught him to exercise pity, that he saved Smith from death, and next day sent him in safety to his friends at Jamestown.

11. It was about eight years after the settlement of Virginia, that is, in 1615, some Dutch adventurers, from Holland, in Europe, made a settlement on the island of New York, which was then called Manhattan. This laid the foundation of the city of New York.

12. In the year 1620, some English people, called Puritans, arrived at Plymouth, in Massachusetts, and made the first settlement in New England.

Who made a settlement on the island of New York?
When was this done?
What was the island of New York called?
What city did the settlement of York Island lay the foundation of?
When did the Puritans come to America?
Where did they arrive?
What settlement did the Puritans make?

13. They came to America, principally, freely to enjoy their own peculiar religion. They were about one hundred in number.

14. The place where they happened to land had been deserted by the Indians, on account of a fatal disease that had prevailed there some years before.

CHAPTER XVIII.

Parley continues to tell of the Settlements of North America.

1. THE Puritans divided themselves into nineteen families, and each family built a small house. Several Indians had been discovered in the woods, but they fled as the white people came near them.

What did they come to America for?
How many of these Puritans were there?
How did they divide themselves?

2. But one day an Indian came among them, and surprised them by exclaiming, "Welcome, Englishmen! Welcome, Englishmen!"

3. His name was Samoset; he had learned to speak English of some fishermen, that he had seen. He was a good friend to the English, and persuaded Masassoit to come and see them.

4. Masassoit was a great chief, or Indian king, and he made an agreement with the English to be at peace with them, and not to injure them.

5. I have now told you of the three first settlements made in North America—Virginia, New York, and New England. These settlements were called colonies.

What surprised the Puritans one day ?
What was this Indian's name ?
How had he learned English?
What did he persuade Masassoit to do?
Who was Masassoit ?
What were the settlements in North America called ?

6. They met with a great many difficulties; sometimes they were afflicted with fatal sickness; sometimes their crops of grain were cut short, and they were visited with famine; sometimes they were involved in the miseries of a war with the Indians.

7. But, notwithstanding all these trials, these colonies flourished, and others were established.

8. In 1621, the first settlement was made in Delaware, by some people from Sweden and Finland, called Swedes and Fins.

9. In 1634, Lord Baltimore, in England, sent out a colony of Roman Catholics, who settled Maryland.

10. In 1681, William Penn, a Quaker, made a settlement of Quakers in Pennsylvania.

Will you describe their difficulties?

When, and by whom, was the first settlement made in Delaware?

When, and by whom, was Maryland settled?

When, and by whom, was the first settlement in Pennsylvania made?

11. Thus, you see, in the space of a few years after the settlement of Virginia, a large portion of what is now called the United States was inhabited ; and, the settlement of the country thus begun, it flourished and increased beyond what has ever been known in any other country.

CHAPTER XIX.

Parley talks about the Settlement of North America, and the Old French War.

1. You will readily understand, that the people, who lived in those days, were very differently situated from what we are now.

2. If you look on the map, you will see it filled with the names of towns, and crossed in every direction by roads.

What will you see if you look on a map of the United States ?

3. One hundred and fifty years ago, very few of these towns existed. The land, where they now stand, lay buried in forests.

4. If you were to travel through the country now, you would see fine houses, gardens, orchards, and cultivated fields. Their place was then occupied by a vast wilderness.

5. Now, there are stages and steamboats, which will carry you rapidly from one end of the country to the other.

6. Then, there were no roads, or very indifferent ones, and travelling was attended with danger from the Indians, and the wild beasts, that lurked in the forests.

7. You see, then, how much happier our condition is than that of our forefathers; and

---

What can you say of the existence of these towns 150 years ago?
What was there, where these towns are now?
What would you now see if you were to travel through the United States?
What will now carry people from one end of the country to the other?
What was the state of the country, in respect to travelling, 150 years ago?
Is our condition happier than that of our forefathers?

how do you think the change, that we have just noticed, and for which we owe so much to our ancestors, has been accomplished?

8. How have the forests been levelled, and made to give place to fruitful fields? How have large and splendid cities been built? How have convenient and pleasant roads been made?

9. How have the wild beasts been subdued? How have the Indians been driven over the mountains? How, in short, has a wild wilderness been converted into a beautiful and happy land?

10. It would take me a long time to answer all these questions. I have only time to tell you, in general, that this great and happy change has been effected by the industry, courage and virtue of our forefathers.

How has the great change that has taken place in America since its settlement been effected?

11. Let me recommend it to you, as soon as you can, to read the history of our country. You will find it very interesting, and it will tell you the whole story of what I have just been talking about.

12. I must now pass over a long period of time, during which our country rapidly advanced in numbers and power, and come to the year 1756.

13. This was the period of a celebrated war, in this country, called the Old French War.

14. You will recollect that this country was settled by English people, and belonged to England.

15. The French had made some settlements in Canada, on the north, and along the rivers

---

When was the Old French war ?
Who settled this country, and to what country did it belong ?
Where had the French made some settlements ?

Mississippi and Ohio, on the west, while the English had been forming the settlements along the Atlantic shore.

16. Well, France and England fell into a state of war. It is always the object of two nations engaged in war to do to each other as much harm as possible, and to conquer and take possession of each other's lands or territories, if they can.

17. To promote these objects, their soldiers do not hesitate to kill the people, burn the houses, and destroy the property of such countries as they are at war with.

18. Whatever belongs, therefore, to a country at war with another, is exposed to all the evils which such a state of things may threaten.

19. Now, the principal settlements, or col-

What happened to France and England ?
What is always the object of two countries at war ?
What is all that belongs to a country at war with another, exposed to ?

onies in North America, belonged to England; of course the French would endeavour to do them all the mischief in their power, and conquer them, if possible. The English would, in like manner, exert themselves to annoy, distress, and conquer the French colonies in Canada, and along the Ohio and Mississippi.

CHAPTER XX.

Parley tells of the Old French War.

1. ACCORDINGLY, when the war broke out between England and France, the people of the French and English colonies began to fight each other.

2. The French engaged large numbers of Indians to assist them, and, instigated by

What would the French endeavour to do to the English colonies ?
What would the English exert themselves to do to the French colonies ?
What happened when the war broke out in 1756 ?
What did the French do respecting the Indians in this war ?

malice toward the English, for having got possession of their lands, they committed the most cruel and inhuman outrages. Here is a picture of one of the scenes of this war.

3. But of these outrages I cannot tell you more now; I can only describe to you the

What was the consequence ?

capture of Quebec, which was the most remarkable event of the war.

4. This city was the capital of the French
settlements in Canada, and is now a large
town. It was strongly fortified, and defended
by a large army, commanded by a brave
French officer, whose name was Montcalm.

5. But General Wolfe, commander of the
English army, was a very bold general, and
he determined to attack them.

6. The French army, consisting of a large
number of men, occupied the garrisons and
forts in and about Quebec.

7. Near the city, and overlooking it, was a

What was the most remarkable event of this war ?
What can you say of Quebec ?
Who commanded the army that defended Quebec ?
Who commanded the English army ?
What sort of a general was Montcalm ?
What sort of a general was Wolfe ?
What did the French army occupy ?
How are the Heights of Abraham situated ?

lofty hill or eminence, called the Heights of Abraham.

8. Wolfe, having made several unsuccessful attacks on the French, determined, if possible, to form his army on the top of these heights.

9. Accordingly, in the night, his soldiers climbed up the hill, and in the morning were ready for battle.

10. About ten o'clock, the conflict began. You have never seen a battle, and can scarce imagine what it is.

11. You must conceive thousands of soldiers, divided into two great portions, with swords, and guns, and cannon.

12. At length the two armies approach each other, and the contest begins. The muskets are fired, and the cannon are discharged.

What did Wolfe determine to do ?
What, accordingly, did his soldiers do ?
At what time did the conflict begin ?
Describe a battle.

13. The whole scene is wrapped in a cloud of thick smoke, through which you can see a thousand flashes, and from which there issues an incessant and deafening roar.

14. By and by, there is a momentary pause; the cloud of smoke is slowly lifted up on the air, and you see the field strewed with the bodies of the men that are dying and dead.

15. Again the battle begins; again the smoke covers the fight; and again the thunder of artillery is heard.

16. Such was the battle on the Heights of Abraham. The French army made a brave onset upon the English, but they were cut down in hundreds.

17. Again and again they returned to the attack, but in vain. The English still maintained their ground, and the French were beaten, and obliged to fly.

18. The brave General Wolfe was wound-

ed, and died on the field of battle. Montcalm, the French general, was also wounded, and died in a short time.

19. The victory was proclaimed in favour of the English. A thousand Frenchmen were killed, and a thousand were taken prisoners.

20. In five days after the victory, Quebec was surrendered, or given up, to the English, and ever since has belonged to them.

21. It was during this war, and not long after the surrender of Quebec, that Montreal and the other French possessions in Canada were taken by the English, and have ever since remained in their possession.

What was the fate of General Wolfe in the battle at Quebec ?
What was the fate of Montcalm ?
In whose favour was the victory proclaimed ?
How many Frenchmen were killed ? How many taken prisoners ?
In how many days after the battle was Quebec given up to the English ?
To whom has Quebec ever since belonged ?
When was it that the French possessions in Canada were taken by the English ?
To whom have they belonged since ?

CHAPTER XXI.

Parley tells about the Revolution.

1. But I must now relate to you the most interesting part of our history ; I mean the revolutionary war. But, before I can make you fully understand this, I must add a few explanations.

2. You will remember, that the English settlements in North America were called *colonies*, that is, they were subject to the government of England, and formed part of its dominions.

3. The people acknowledged the authority of the king, and paid obedience to him, and expected, of course, his protection.

What is the most interesting part of our history ?
What were the English settlements in America called ?
What government were they subject to ?
Whose authority did the people acknowledge ?
What did they of course expect from the king ?

4. But it happened, that the king and government of England were unjust to the colonies.

5. They made laws, and imposed burdens, which were calculated to injure the people in this country. In short, they acted towards it without regard to the rights and the happiness of the people, and sought only their own immediate advantage.

6 Their idea was, that the colonies were weak and timid, and that they would submit to any thing, however oppressive, that the government of England should require of them. In this, you will see, they were greatly mistaken.

7. As the colonies had been protected by

What was the conduct of the king and government of England toward the colonies ?

What kind of laws did they make ?

How, in short, did they act towards this country ?

What was their idea ?

England; as many of the people had been born and educated there; and as nearly the whole of them were descended from English ancestors, the attachment of the colonists to England was very strong.

8. England seemed to them their home, and all of us, you know, are fond of home.

9. They therefore endured much oppression from the English government, contenting themselves with only sending to the king earnest prayers, that he would treat them with kindness and justice.

10. But as no answer was returned to these prayers, save that of increased hardships, the people resolved that they would no longer acknowledge the right of England to rule over them, and that they would govern themselves.

What can you say of the attachment of the people in America to England?
What, therefore, did they endure?
With what did the colonies content themselves?
What followed their prayers?
On what did the people resolve?

11. Accordingly, the people sent some of their wisest men to Philadelphia. These men, when assembled, were called a congress.

12. This congress, on the fourth of July, 1776, declared that the people of this country would no longer submit to the government of Great Britain, and that ever after they should be free and independent.

13. This is called the declaration of independence; and it is celebrated every year, on the fourth of July, that being the day on which the declaration was made. Thus the colonies became an independent nation.

14. But before that independence was established, and before it was acknowledged by

---

What, accordingly, did the people do?

What did the congress do?

When did they make this declaration?

What is this declaration called?

When is it celebrated?

What did the colonies thus become?

Great Britain, our fathers had to pass through a bloody war, which lasted for eight years. The story of this war I will now tell you.

CHAPTER XXII.

The Story of the Revolutionary War.

1. THE revolutionary war began in 1775 The English government, fearing that the people of America would resist their authority, sent a large number of soldiers to prevent it. These soldiers were placed in Boston.

2. It happened, that there were some military stores, that is, powder, ball, guns, &c., at Concord, about sixteen miles from Boston.

How long did the war of the Revolution last ?
When did this war begin ?
What did the English government do ?
Where were their soldiers placed ?
What happened to be at Concord ?

Governor Gage, the English commander, wished to have those stores destroyed, as they belonged to the Americans.

3. Accordingly, he sent some soldiers, on the nineteenth of April, 1775, to effect their destruction. When these soldiers got to Lexington, on their way to Concord, they found a good many people, alarmed by the expedition, gathered about the church.

4. One of the English officers, Major Pitcairn, rode up to these people, and exclaimed-"Disperse, you rebels!" At the same time, some of his soldiers fired upon the people, and

What did Governor Gage wish ?

Who was Governor Gage ?

What did he do ?

What did these soldiers find when they got to Lexington ?

What did Major Pitcairn do ?

What did some of the English soldiers do ?

killed a number of them.   Here is a picture
of the scene.

5. Now the Americans did not like to have
their people killed by foreign soldiers.   Would
it not make you angry, if soldiers should come
from England, and shoot your dear father or
your brother?

Certainly it would ; and so the Americans were excited to resistance by this act of the English soldiers, and they determined to resent and revenge it.

7. They ran to their houses; they seized their guns, and, hurrying back in crowds, they commenced a sharp attack upon the English troops.

8. These soon found it necessary to turn about, and fly to Boston for safety. The Americans pursued them, and the English soldiers, urged by the danger which their own acts had drawn down upon them, pushed on with a rapid step, and soon reached Boston.

9. This affair began the revolutionary war. The people now saw the necessity of resistance.

What were the Americans excited to by the expedition of the English soldiers to Lexington?

What did they do?

What did the English troops find it necessary to do?

What did they do?

What did the Lexington affair begin?

What necessity did the people now see?

10. Animated by a love of their country, and roused by indignation against its oppressors, they left their quiet homes, bade adieu to their families, and, with a resolute purpose of securing their country's rights, they flocked to the field of battle.

11. The British troops being stationed in Boston, the Americans assembled their forces in that neighbourhood.

12. I had at this time grown up to be a man, and lived in Boston. The British troops had possession of the town, and it was difficult for me to leave it. But I was determined to join the American forces.

13. It was expected that there would soon be a great battle. There is a high hill near

---

By what were they animated ?
Thus animated, what did they do ?
Where were the British troops stationed ?
Where did the Americans assemble their soldiers ?
What was it expected would soon take place ?

Boston, called Bunker's Hill.   The top of
this hill you can see from Boston.

14. One morning it was discovered that the
American troops had got possession of the hill,
and, during the night, had thrown up a small
breastwork of earth and turf.

15. Governor Gage immediately perceived
that he must drive the Americans from this
hill, if possible.   Accordingly, the English
troops were ordered to proceed to the spot.

16. That was a busy morning in Boston.
The people hurried along the streets with
breathless haste, and countenances of deep
anxiety.

17. Heavy columns of troops poured along
the town, and the deep swell of martial mu-

What high hill can you see from Boston ?
What was discovered one morning ?
What did Governor Gage perceive ?
What were the English troops, accordingly, ordered to do ?
What did the people of Boston do that morning ?

sic filled the air. Amid all this, a heavy sound of cannon, at no great distance, was distinctly heard.

CHAPTER XXIII.

Parley continues to tell of the American Revolution.

1. I COULD remain inactive no longer. I proceeded with three of my companions, among whom was James Jenkins, to a spot where we had secreted a small boat, in which we rowed over to Cambridge.

2. Here we landed, and proceeded to join the troops on the top of the hill. From this place we could see the British forces as they approached.

3. They landed on a point at no great dis-

What was seen and heard?

What did Parley now do in company with James Jenkins?

Where did they proceed to?

Where did the British troops land?

tance from us. They were soon formed, and began their march up the hill.

4. Nothing could exceed the regularity with which they approached. They were all dressed in red coats and white pantaloons. It was a bright day, and their guns glittered in the sun.

5. In long, straight lines, and with a bold and steady march, they advanced toward the breastwork, behind which the Americans lay.

6. Jenkins and myself were among them, side by side. It was an anxious moment. Not a word was said. We lay with our guns loaded, and our fingers placed ready to send the bullets in the face of the approaching enemy.

7. We saw them; they were so near, that

In what manner did the British troops advance ?
How were they dressed ?
How did they advance ?
How were the American troops situated ?
How did the American troops lie ?

8

we could look them in the face.   Yet not a word was said.   We felt their heavy tread shake the little mound behind which we lay.

8. Now the signal was given; every gun was levelled, and an instantaneous blaze ran like lightning along the breastwork.   More than a thousand muskets poured their deadly shot upon the very breast of the British line.

9. The effect was astounding; many an English soldier was stretched instantly on the earth, and the remainder first wavered, and then turned, and fled from the deadly spot.

10. But the English troops soon formed, and renewed the attack.   It was answered as before, and again they retired.   But, at length, the Americans, having exhausted their powder and ball, were forced to retreat.

When the signal was given, what happened ?

What was the effect ?

But what did the English troops soon do ?

What happened in consequence of the Americans having exhausted their powder and ball ?

11. With slow and reluctant steps, they descended from the hill, leaving the British in possession of it. Many of the English were killed, and but very few of the Americans. This was the famous battle of Bunker's Hill. Here is a picture of it.

What did the Americans do?
Wha. battle was this?

12. Now the war was begun in earnest. The Americans set about making arrangements to defend themselves, and, if possible, drive the British troops from the country.

13. They accordingly appointed George Washington, a wise and brave man, to command the American forces, and took measures to raise a large and powerful army.

14. At the same time, the king of England, filled with resentment, and resolving to subdue the rebellious colonies, sent a great many ships, and many thousands of soldiers, to assist in accomplishing his wishes.

What did the Americans now set about doing?

Whom did they appoint to command the American army?

What was the character of Washington?

What did the king of England do at the same time?

CHAPTER XXIV.

Parley tells of his strange Adventures among the Indians.

1. I CANNOT now tell you of all the battles that were fought during this bloody war, but I will tell you an interesting story of what happened to myself. It was a little more than two years after the battle of Bunker's Hill. Jenkins and myself had been stationed at a small fort in the state of New York, on the shore of Lake Ontario.

2. We determined to accompany a detachment which was going to join the American troops under General Gates, who were then

---

Where had Parley and Jenkins been stationed after the battle of Bunker' Hill?

Will you tell me the story of Parley's being taken by the Indians? If you will learn it by heart, you can repeat it all.

near Saratoga, and who soon expected to meet a large British army advancing from Canada, under General Burgoyne.

3. Accordingly we set out. The detachment consisted of about sixty men. The second day after our departure, as we were passing along a sort of military road, cut through the woods, we were startled by the report of a musket from an adjacent thicket.

4. The sun had set a little before, and it was now nearly dark. We could, of course, see no one in the woods, nor had we suspected that an enemy could be near us.

5. We had no doubt, however, that the shot proceeded from Indians, who were lurking in the woods, and who were about to attack us.

6. It happened at the moment, that Jenkins and myself were marching together a few

rods behind the other men. The instant I heard the report of the musket, I saw Jenkins stop, and lay his hand quickly upon his side.

7. I sprung towards him, knowing that the bullet had wounded him. I was a momen too late to prevent his falling!

8. I put my arms around him, and raised his head. He instantly exclaimed, "I am wounded, and must die: leave me! The Indians are around us; their next bullet will go through your heart: join the troops, and save yourself!"

9. I had not time to answer, for four Indians at the moment sprung from the bushes, seized me, and hurried me from the spot. I had no time for resistance; the whole scene passed in an instant.

10. I exerted myself a little to try the strength of my captors, but found that I was

strongly grasped by two stout men, one on each side.

11. It was dark, and I could only perceive that they were savages, and that they were urging me through a forest of tall trees without underwood.

12. After proceeding at this rapid pace for about a quarter of an hour, we stopped, and my hands were bound behind me.

13. We then pressed on as before, and my speed was occasionally increased by a rude push from the savages. In this way we travelled about an hour, when we again stopped.

14. The Indians, who had been silent before, now began to talk to themselves. After some apparent consultation, they permitted me to sit down, and sat down themselves.

15 Having remained about two hours, we

were joined by a dozen more Indians. In company with these, we now resumed our march, and went forward at a rapid pace.

16. As we were travelling through woods, in the night, my hands being tied behind me, I found it extremely difficult to keep up with the Indians, and whenever I faltered, they did not fail to strike me.

17. At length the morning began to dawn, and we made a halt. The Indians, who had hitherto spoken in their own language, now asked me a few questions in English.

18. In return, I made some inquiries of them, which they refused to answer. All that I could learn respecting my own fate was, that I should be reserved for the decision of their chief, who would arrive the next day.

19. In the mean time, as if to torment me, they tied me to a tree, and some of the young

F

Indians tried their skill in shooting arrows at me. Here is a picture of the scene.

CHAPTER XXV.

Parley's Adventures continued.

1. SEVERAL of the arrows came very near me, and one or two of them hit me, and wounded me, but not very severely.

2. When the arrows hit me, the Indians laughed very heartily, and my misery seemed to afford them great pleasure.

3. I should have been in despair, and given myself up for lost, but I had often before been in danger, and had always escaped.

4. I had also found, that danger, when met with courage, seemed to be lessened, and that evils, sustained with resolution, always disappeared or diminished.

5. I placed confidence in Heaven, too, and felt persuaded that a kind Providence would rescue me.

6. So I bore the wounds of the Indians' arrows with fortitude, and could not but scorn and pity the wretches who took delight in my distress.

7. At length they seemed weary of their cruel sport, and left me tied to the tree, while they went to their meals.

8. After finishing this, they offered me some broiled deer's flesh, but I was too closely tied to permit me to eat.

9. They then unbound me, but my hands were so swollen that I could not use them. I was very hungry, however, and was able to eat a little.

10. At length night came on. I had resolved, if possible, to escape during the night.

11. The chief was expected the next morning, and, from what I knew of the Indians, I had little doubt that I should be burned to death when he came, unless I could get away before his return.

12. I determined, therefore, to avail myself of the least chance of escape, if any should offer.

13. The place where we were was a high, rocky bank of a small river.   My plan was to

escape silently, if I could, when all were asleep.

14. If that could not be done, I intended to spring suddenly from my keepers, and leap over the rocks into the river, hoping, if I was not dashed to pieces, to elude pursuit in the darkness, and make good my escape.

15. With these purposes in my mind, I waited impatiently for the time when the savages should be asleep.

16. It was midnight before they were at rest. I was strongly bound, and laid on the ground, with about twelve Indians around me.

17. At length they all seemed asleep. I then exerted myself to break the bark cords that tied me. I had nearly succeeded, when one of the Indians suddenly sprung up, and came towards me with a hatchet lifted over my head.

18. I expected that he would strike me, but

he did not. He examined my cords, and, as they seemed to be tight, and as I appeared to be asleep, he left me, and laid himself again on the ground.

19. Soon all were asleep. Now, thought I, is the moment which decides whether I live or die! I made a desperate effort, and broke the cords around my hands.

20. I then untied those that were around my feet, and stepped cautiously over the sleeping Indians.

21. One of them muttered in his sleep, and stirred, as if he was going to wake, but he did not. I took one of the Indians' muskets, which stood by a tree, and with a noiseless step, and breathless anxiety, I left the spot.

22. I had not been gone more than a quarter of an hour, when I heard a shout among the Indians, which was immediately followed

by a mingled yell, that echoed through the forest.

23. I now knew that my escape was discovered. I was on the bank of the river, and surrounded by rocks. I crept between two large rocks, and lay still. I soon heard the Indians coming in the direction where I was.

24. Two or three passed so close to me that I could have touched them with my hand. At length one of them saw me, and levelled his musket at me, but hesitated to fire.

25. I took advantage of the moment, and sprung over the bank into the river. I swam across the stream, carrying the musket in one hand, and paddling with the other.

26. I had scarcely got across, when I heard two or three savages plash into the opposite side of the water.

27. I climbed up the steep bank, and, plunging into the woods, I ran with all my force.

But I was stiff from my wounds, and from having been so tightly bound.

28. Of course, the swift Indians soon overtook me, and I was again reduced to captivity. I was now taken back to the place from which I had escaped, and bound, but more securely than before.

CHAPTER XXV.

Parley's Adventures continued.

1. At length the morning came, and the chief of the tribe arrived, with several other Indians. He was an old man, but still strong and active.

2. The Indians told him of my capture and attempt to escape, and asked him what should be my fate. Having heard the story, he came near to me, and, in a stern voice, he spoke as follows:

3. "White man," said he, "listen to me! Once the red man was king over these woods and waters. The mountains and rivers were then the red man's, and then he was rich and happy.

4. "At length the white men, thy fathers, came. The red man bade them welcome. But they were ungrateful and treacherous.

5. "When they grew strong, they drove the red men over the mountains, and took their lands. I was still the white man's friend.

6. "But see here," said he, pointing to a scar on his breast; "this is the mark of a white man's bullet. I had harmed them not; I had lived among them, and served them. But they shot at me as if I were a wild cat.

7. "White man," said he, "listen. I was once the white man's friend; I am now his enemy. Think no more of escape. This hour you shall die."

8. "Chief," said I, "do as you like! If it

9

is God's will that I die, I shall die contented. My father was a friend to the red men, and his son has never harmed them.

9. " My father saved the life of a red man, and now you will kill his son.   If it will make an Indian chief happy to spill the blood of one, whose father saved a red man's life, then kill me; I am ready to die.

10. "And my soul will go to the Great Spirit, and will say to him, 'My father was a benefactor to the red men, and they murdered his son!' "

11. "Speak," said the chief; "where did your father live?" " In Boston," said I. " And who was the Indian, whose life he saved?" "His name was Wampum," I replied.

12. "White man," said he, "look at me! I am Wampum!   I know you; you were the boy who came to my wigwam at Holyoke. You were the boy who went with me to the great

Falls. It was your father who saved my life, and shall I suffer his son to die?

13. "Brethren," said Wampum, speaking to the Indians, "I was a stranger in a distant city of the white men. I drank their fire-water,* and it made me wild.

14. "I struck a sailor, and he was angry. He came upon me with twelve men. They beat me down, and trampled upon me. They would have killed me, but a white man, with a strong arm, beat them off. The friend of the red men saved my life. Here is his son, shall he die?"

15. The Indians answered by unbinding my hands and feet. "Go," said Wampum, "go to your friends, and tell them that the red men will not forget kindness.

16. "Tell them, that we will repay to the children the good deeds of their fathers. We

---

* The Indians call rum "fire-water."

war only with the wicked; we seek only the blood of our enemies."

17. Saying this, he returned me my gun, gave me a bag of dried deer's flesh, and told me I was at liberty to go. "Keep along the bank of this river," said he, "and three days' journey will bring you to the American camp."

18. Having expressed my thankfulness to the chief, I departed. I found no difficulty in proceeding along the banks of the river. I travelled all day without accident. At night I made a little fire, and slept by it.

19. The next day I proceeded on my journey, and at evening found myself among wild hills and rocks, between which the river dashed in violent cascades.

20. I was looking about for a place to sleep during the night, when I perceived a man approaching me. His face was pale, and wore a look of strange wildness.

21. What was my astonishment to discover this to be James Jenkins, whom I had supposed killed three days before!

22. He told me he had been left on the ground for dead, but was only wounded. He had lain on the spot a night and day, and since that time had wandered about in the woods.

23. He was very weak from hunger and loss of blood; but, after eating some of my dried deer's flesh, he slept quietly through the night, and found himself able to accompany me, the next morning, on my journey, at a slow pace.

24. In three days we arrived at the American camp, and joined our regiment under the command of General Gates.

25. I hope my little readers will learn this story, so that they can tell it all without the book.

CHAPTER XXVII.

Parley tells more about the Revolutionary War.

1. It was now a time of great interest in the army. General Burgoyne, the English commander, with about six thousand men, lay at no great distance.

2. There had been a good deal of fighting between this army and the American forces under General Gates.

3. About a month after Jenkins and I had arrived, the two armies met. They fought for a long time, and many hundreds were killed, but neither was decidedly victorious.

4. General Burgoyne was now surrounded with difficulties, and was soon obliged to sur-

Who was General Burgoyne?

How many men had he under his command?

What happened about a month after Parley and Jenkins arrived at the camp?

How was General Burgoyne now situated?

render, and give himself up, with his six thousand soldiers, to General Gates, who made them prisoners of war.

5. These events, you will remember, took place near Saratoga, in the state of New York, in the fall of 1777.

6. This was a great event for the Americans, and gave them courage to prosecute the war with spirit.

7. I should be glad to tell you of the many battles that were fought, and of the many brave deeds that were done, by the Americans.

8. You will some time or other read the history of these things, and will admire the noble spirit of your fathers.

9. To their courage and fortitude, you, who now live and enjoy happiness, peace and freedom, are indebted for these blessings.

What did General Burgoyne do?
Where did these events happen?
When did they happen?
What effect had this on the Americans?

10. Let their example never be forgotten; and if your country should ever again be invaded by enemies, be sure to imitate the conduct of those who forgot every private interest and feeling in the ardent desire to protect their country.

11. After the capture of Burgoyne, I left the army, and returned to Boston. Here I remained till the fall of 1781.

12. I then joined the army, and was present at the capture of the British army at Yorktown, under Lord Cornwallis.

13. This was the greatest and most important event of the revolutionary war. The circumstances were these.

14. Lord Cornwallis, at the head of seven thousand British troops, was at Yorktown, Virginia. To this place General Washington

Where was Lord Cornwallis when he was captured with the British army ? How many British troops had he ?
Who marched against the British at the head of the American army ?

marched, at the head of the American army, determined, if possible, to overcome and capture the British.

15. He soon began the attack, and, in a few days, Lord Cornwallis, with his seven thousand soldiers, gave themselves up to Genera Washington. Here is a picture of the scene.

16. This was the last great event of the

What did Washington do?
What did Lord Cornwallis do?

war. England now saw that she could not conquer America. Accordingly she gave up the idea, and acknowledged its independence.

17. Such was the war called the American Revolution. Our country's independence being thus secured, it has gone on in happiness and prosperity. It has once since been engaged in war with England, but that lasted only a short time, and terminated honourably to our country.

CHAPTER XXVIII·

Conclusion.

1. Ours is now a great and powerful nation. It is called the United States of Amer-

---

What did England now perceive? What, accordingly, did she do? What has happened to America since her independence was secured? Has it been since involved in war? With what country? Is not ours now a great and powerful nation? What is it called?

ica, and contains eleven millions of people. They are governed by a President and Congress, who meet every winter, at Washington, to make laws.

2. The Congress consists of several hundred men, some from each state, who assemble in a building called the Capitol.

3. The United States now embraces twenty-four states, each separate and distinct, having a governor of its own, yet all united under the general government of the President and Congress.

4. The names of these states are as follows: Maine, New Hampshire, Vermont, Massachu

How is our country governed?
Where does Congress meet?
What does Congress meet for?
Of what does Congress consist?
Where does Congress assemble?
How many separate states are there now in the United States?
Does each state have a separate governor?
What are the names of those states called New England?

setts, Rhode Island, and Connecticut. These states, taken together, are usually called New England.

5. New York, New Jersey, Pennsylvania, and Delaware, are usually called the Middle States.

6. Virginia, North Carolina, South Carolina, Georgia, Alabama, Maryland, and Mississippi, are called the Southern States.

7. Ohio, Tennessee, Kentucky, Indiana, Illinois, Louisiana, and Missouri, are called the Western States.

8. I have now almost finished my stories about America. I have told you how Columbus discovered America; how Cortez conquered Mexico, and Pizarro Peru.

9. You will recollect that I have told you of

What are the names of the Middle States?

The Southern? The Western?

Will you repeat, or tell over, the principal things I have told you about America?

the settlement of Virginia, New York, New England, Delaware, Maryland and Pennsylvania, and that I have described the French war, and the revolutionary war.

10. These things I hope you will never forget; but, lest you should, I will put them into rhymes for you, which, if you please, you may commit to memory, and recite to your friends.

———◆———

CHAPTER XXIX.

The Story of America in Verse.

COLUMBUS was a sailor brave,
The first that crossed th' Atlantic wave.
In fourteen hundred ninety-two,
He came far o'er the ocean blue,
Where ne'er a ship had sailed before,
And found a wild and savage shore,

Where naked men in forests prowled,
And bears and panthers roamed and howled.

Then others came to see the wonder,
To gather gold and seek for plunder ;
And many a cruel deed was done,
Far south, beneath the tropic sun.
There Cortez came, with sword and flame,
   And, at a blow, proud Mexico
Was humbled in the dust;
   Pizarro, too, in rich Peru,
With bloody heart, and cruel art,
A mighty empire crushed.
Ah ! many a red man's blood was spilt,
And many a deed was done of guilt,
Of torture, murder, crimes untold
To get the poor, poor Indians' gold.

At length, when years had passed away,
Some English came to Virginia ;

'Twas sixteen hundred seven ; be sure
You let this in your mind endure ;
For 'twas the first bold colony
Planted in North America;
The first that laid the deep foundation,
On which has since been built a nation.
Well, here they raised a far-famed town
On James' River, called Jamestown.
They struggled hard 'gainst many sorrows,
Sickness and want, and Indian arrows ;
But bold and strong at length they grew,
And were a brave and manly crew.

'Twas eight years after this,—I mean
The year sixteen hundred fifteen,—
Some Dutch, from Holland, settled pat on
An island which they called Manhattan,
And straight they set themselves to work,
And built the city of New York.

Now let the laughing wags and jokers
Say that the Dutch are stupid smokers;
We only tell, that, dull or witty,
They founded famous New York city;
The largest city in the west,
For trade and commerce quite the best.

Then came along, in five years more,
The Puritans, or pilgrims, o'er;
Be sure the time and month remember—
'Twas the cold season of December.
On Plymouth rock the little band
Of weary wanderers first did land;
And hearty thanks to Heaven they gave,
For kind protection o'er the wave.
The scene was wild, for hill and dale
Were clothed in winter's snowy veil,
And all the shore the eye could mark
Was covered thick with forests dark,

Within whose gloomy shades afar
Was heard the Indian whoop of war.
But bold and strong these pilgrims were,
They feared not Indian, wolf, or bear:
Though far from home, a feeble band,
Unfriended, in a desert land,
Where wild beasts sought at night their prey
And ruthless Indians lurked by day,
By sickness pressed, by want beset,
Each ill they braved, each danger met.
Long, long they strove, and much endured,
To sufferings were long inured;
But naught their courage could subdue:
'Mid want and war their sinews grew,
Their towns increase, their numbers double,
And soon they triumph o'er their trouble

Thus three strong colonies, we see,
Are planted in America;

10   G

New England in the northern part;
New York within the very heart:
While southward, o'er the hills away,
Is seated fair Virginia.

The first rude dangers thus o'ercome,
Others did seek this land for home,
And came like birds in numbers o'er,
Till, far along the eastern shore,
That bounds the blue Atlantic tide,
Village with village proudly vied;
While Swedes and Fins did settle down
In Delaware, and build a town.
To Maryland Lord Baltimore
A colony of papists sent,
In sixteen hundred thirty-four,
Who there did make a settlement;
And William Penn, the grave peace-maker,
Came o'er, with many an honest Quaker,

To Pennsylvania : 'twas done
In sixteen hundred eighty-one.

CHAPTER XXX.

Story of Amer ca in Verse cont nued.

FULL many a tale I now might tell,
Of war and wo that here befell
The colonists; how oft at night
Their sleep was broke by sudden fright ;
Of Indian whoop and cruel knife,
To spill the blood of babe and wife ;
How prowling wolves and hungry bears
Increased their dangers and their cares :
But this I leave : these scenes are o'er :
The Indian sleeps to wake no more ;
The hungry wolf and bear are still,
And peaceful songs our forests fill.

We pass o'er years that rolled away,
And only mention, in our lay,
That, spite of peril, war and bustle,
Our country grew in bone and muscle,
Till seventeen hundred seventy-five,
Three million souls did live and thrive,
Where late the savage reigned supreme
O'er mountain, valley, lake and stream.

'Twas then began that famous fray
'Twixt England and America :
The revolutionary war
'Tis called, and near and far.
It shook the land, from Georgia's plain
Far northward to the bounds of Maine.
At Lexington the conflict rose,
And Yorktown saw it proudly close.
For eight long years the cry of blood
And battle rang o'er field and flood.

O who the woes of war can tell,
And paint its terrors true and well!
Look o'er the land where war is waging,
And see the fearful tempest raging:
The hills and plains in smoke are wound,
And o'er them heaves the cannon's sound;
The musket's rattling peal, the thrum
Of trumpet hoarse and heavy drum,
And cries of hope and fell despair,
And groans of mortal strife, are there.
The fields are strewed with dead and dying,
And o'er them troops of horse are flying,
Trampling beneath their bloody tread
The mangled forms of hurt and dead.

Stay till the solemn strife is done,
And view the field where victory's won.
The trees, and turf, and rocks are scarred,
As if by whirling tempest marred,

And, hushed in death's embraces deep,
Around the gallant soldiers sleep.
O many a bitter tear shall flow
For those who slumber here so low !
The mother's aged limbs shall quake,
The widow's saddened heart shall break,
The loved and lovely sisters mourn,
For these brave men, so pale and torn.

Such are the scenes of war ; and these
Purchased us liberty and peace.
Such was the mighty storm that hurled
A tyrant from this western world,
Chased dark oppression's night away,
And spread fair freedom's glorious day.

Thus ere our liberty was won,
Full many a gallant deed was done,
And many a patriot nobly fell,
To save the land he loved so well.

O let us ever cherish, then,
The memory of those gallant men,
Who gave their life-blood, fresh and free,
To purchase peace and liberty.
And let us ne'er forget the name
That fills the proudest niche of fame,
And shines o'er others like the sun,
Mid moons and stars—GEORGE WASHINGTON.

I would now go on to tell you my adventures after the American war, but I have already told you a long story. If I should meet you again, I will tell you how I became a traveller, and what strange things I saw in Europe, Asia and Africa.

Perhaps some of my readers are not yet tired. If so, they may turn over the leaf and read a little about the American government.

TALES ABOUT GOVERNMENT

—◆—

Parley tells about the President.

I WILL tell my little readers about the president of the
United States.   He lives at Washington.   Washington
is about 450 miles in a southwesterly direction from Boston.   It is about 250 miles from New York, and 150
miles from Philadelphia.

Well, the president lives at Washington in a very large
house.   I suppose you know that he is a man !   I once
knew a little boy who was very anxious to see the president; so he squeezed through the crowd, and there he
saw a tall man with a black dress, very much like a min-
ister.   "That," said the boy's father, "is the president."

Where does the president live ?
How far is Washington from Boston ?   From New York ?   From Philadelphia ?

" Is that the president ? " said the boy, in great surprise ;
" why, 'tis a man ! "

I suppose you would like to know why he is called
president. It is because he *presides* over the nation.
He is like a father, and the people are like his children.
He watches over them. If enemies come against them,
he sees that they are driven away, and he takes care
that the laws are obeyed and the people protected.

We have had in the United States six presidents .
George Washington, John Adams, Thomas Jefferson,
James Madison, James Monroe, and John Quincy Adams. The present president is Andrew Jackson, and
he makes the seventh.

Would you like to know how the president is chosen?
I will tell you. The people in the several states choose
certain men, called presidential electors; these electors
choose a man to be president.

You will wonder, perhaps, how the president can take
care of so large a country as ours, while he is staying at

Why is the president so called ?
How many presidents have we had in the United States?
What are their names ?
Who is our present president ?
Can you tell how the president is chosen ?

Washington.   I will endeavour to make you understand how he is able to do it, by and by.

◆

Parley tells about Government.

Every country must have what is called government. Government is the power which makes and executes the laws.

Laws, you know, are certain rules which require people to be just to each other, and forbid crimes.

If a man finds some money which another has lost, the laws require him to give the money up to the man who lost it.   The laws forbid one man to wound another man; they forbid stealing or theft, robbery, and murder.   If a man does any of these things, the laws require that he should be punished.

Now these laws are necessary for our safety.   If there were no laws, wicked men would steal from us, rob us,

---

What is government?

What are laws?

What do the laws require if a man finds what another has lost?   If a man steals, robs, or murders, what do the laws require should be done with him?

Why are laws necessary?

and perhaps take away our lives. But, being afraid of being punished, they will not be likely to do these wicked things.

Would you like to know how the laws are made? I will tell you. The people of the United States choose certain men called members of congress. These members of congress, as I have told you, assemble every winter at Washington, in a great building called the capitol, There the congress makes laws.

The laws being made, it is necessary, you know, to have somebody see that the people obey them. Now it is the business of the president to do this. Accordingly he appoints certain persons, in various parts of the United States, to attend to this business. In this way it is that the president is able to have the laws executed in all parts of the country.

These affairs of making laws, and putting them in execution, are called government. As I told you before, every country must have a government, else the people will suffer from the crimes of wicked persons.

Can you tell how laws are made?
Who sees that the people obey the laws?
How does the president do this?

There are various kinds of government. In some countries they have kings to govern them, but in this country we are governed by a president and congress.

Thus, you see, congress makes laws, and the president, and persons appointed by him, have them executed or put in force.

I will tell you another thing. Those who make laws are called legislators, which means law-makers, and a body of law-makers is called a legislature. Therefore congress is sometimes called the national legislature.

Parley tells about Governors.

Did you ever see a governor? A governor is like a president, only that a president watches over the affairs of the whole nation, and a governor watches only over the affairs of a single state.

President Jackson presides over the laws made by congress at Washington for the whole country. Governor

How are they governed in some countries ?
How are they governed in this country ?
What are those that make laws called ?
What is congress sometimes called ?
How does a governor differ from a president ?

Lincoln, of Massachusetts, only presides over the laws made by the legislature of Massachusetts.

The president is chosen by all the people of the United States; a governor is chosen by the people of one state

Each state has a government of its own. Each state has a legislature to make laws, and a governor to see them executed.

The legislature of a state consists of persons chosen by the people of the several towns in a state. They meet together, and make laws for their own state. The laws made in one state have no force in another state.

For example, the laws made by the legislature of New York have no force in Pennsylvania, nor in any state except New York. The laws made by congress operate all over the United States.

Parley tells about Courts.

Courts are established to try people who are accused of breaking the laws.

Has each state a governor?
What does the legislature of a state consist of?
Are the laws made in one state good in another?
Where do the laws made by congress operate?
What are courts established for?

There is, for example, a law against theft or stealing, Now if a man is said to have been guilty of theft, he is brought before a court   The court consists of men called judges.   These judges examine into the case.   If the man is found guilty, that is, if he is proved to have committed theft, he is punished.

Sometimes a man is punished by being shut up in a prison or jail.   If a man is found guilty of murder, he is hanged by the neck till he is dead.

Thus, you see, it is very dangerous to break the laws, because, a man who breaks them is put in prison, or hanged, or punished some other way.

In this way wicked men are made afraid to break the laws.   They are afraid to do injury to others, because, if they do so, they will be punished.

I hope my little readers will be afraid to break the laws because it is wicked, and not merely because it is dangerous.

Parley tells about a Robber.

THERE was a man riding one night through a forest.   Suddenly a person sprung from the woods, seized

---

What do courts consist of?

Suppose a man is found guilty, how is he sometimes punished ?

his horse's bridle, and commanded him to give up his money.

The man refused to do it. The robber shot a pistol at the traveller, and wounded him. The man fell from his horse to the ground. The robber then took the traveller's money, and fled.

The traveller was able to get upon his horse again, and give notice of the robbery. The robber was taken. He was carried before a court. The court examined the facts, and the man was proved guilty. He was then put in a strong prison, where he was kept at hard work for twenty years.

Parley tells about War.

Two nations frequently go to war with each other. Nations at war send soldiers to kill the people, burn the houses, and destroy the property of their enemies.

Now suppose the king of England should make war on this country. He would send soldiers here, to kill the people, burn our houses, and destroy our property.

What do nations at war do ?

What could be done in such a case to defend the people? Why, the president must send soldiers to fight the soldiers sent by the king of England, and drive them away.

Thus, you see, it is the duty of the president, not only to watch over the people by seeing that the laws are obeyed, but it is also his duty to see that the people are defended in time of war.

It is important that the president should be a very wise and good man. If he is not so, the people may suffer very much.

What is the duty of the president in time of war?
What ought the president to be?